FIRST EDITION

Copyright © 1989
By Joe Tom Davis

Published in the United States of America
By Eakin Press, P.O. Box 23069, Austin, Texas 78735

ISBN 0-89015-669-7

Library of Congress Cataloging-in-Publication Data
(Revised for Vol. IV)

Davis, Joe Tom, 1942–
    Legendary Texians.

    Includes bibliographies and indexes.
    1. Texas — Biography — Juvenile literature. 2. Frontier and pioneer life
— Texas — Juvenile literature. 3. Texas — History — Juvenile Literature.
I. Title
CT262.D38   1982   976.4'009'92   [B]   84-18685
ISBN 0-89015-336-1 (Vol. I)
ISBN 0-89015-473-2 (Vol. II)
ISBN 0-89015-559-3 (Vol. III)
ISBN 0-89015-669-7 (Vol. IV)

This book is dedicated to
Kathy
and her children,
Stephanie, Thornton,
and Sarah Menefee

About the Author

Joe Tom Davis is a fifth-generation Texan. His maternal great-great-grandfather, George Lord, was a survivor of the Mier Expedition and the "Lottery of Death."

Davis attended public schools at Edna, Texas. He later became a navy veteran and earned two degrees from Sam Houston State University, where he was elected to Alpha Chi, Who's Who, and received the James Ellison Kirkley Prize as outstanding social science student. After teaching at Sam Houston for two years, he joined the faculty of Wharton County Junior College in 1965 as an instructor of American and Texas history.

While teaching at the junior college, Davis has been elected to Outstanding Educators of America and is a leader in campus beautification efforts. He has a special interest in singing and is a choir member and Sunday school teacher at First Baptist Church, El Campo.

A noted public speaker in the area of Texas history, Davis won a statewide award from the Texas Historical Commission in 1987 for his work in oral history television interviews. He is a member of the Texas State Historical Association and the Texas Junior College Teachers Association.

Davis has written three other books: *Legendary Texians,* Volume I (1982), Volume II (1985), and Volume III (1986), all published by Eakin Press.

Contents

Acknowledgments   vii

Introduction   ix

I **"Three-Legged Willie" Williamson:**
A Legend in His Own Time   1

II **Jack Hays:**
He Fought the Good Fight   30

III **Richard King:**
Founder of a Ranching Empire   89

IV **Sul Ross:**
Warrior, Public Servant, and Educator   148

Suggested Sources for Further Reading   195

Index   199

Acknowledgments

This book could not have been written without the assistance of my colleagues and friends. I am especially grateful for the wonderful support I received from Mrs. Patsy L. Norton, director of the J. M. Hodges Learning Center at Wharton County Junior College, and her able staff. Much of my reading and research was done in the Hodges Learning Center, where an extensive collection of Texas history titles has been acquired since 1964 through the generosity of the Raymond Dickson Foundation and proceeds from the book *The History of Wharton County,* by Annie Lee Williams. When I needed an interlibrary loan, the Learning Center staff was always prompt in obtaining the reference materials. I am truly fortunate that Assistant Director J. C. Hoke is also an accomplished photographer. Mr. Hoke provided on-site photos for this book, along with numerous photographic reproductions. The outstanding quality of his work enhances the worth and appeal of the book.

I also wish to thank two members of the college English Department, Dr. Sandra Coats and the late Mr. R. L. Cowser, Jr., for advising me on matters of punctuation and usage. The words of encouragement and praise I received from Mr. Nicholas Miller, chairman of the History Department, have been deeply appreciated. For illustrations, I am indebted to Mrs. Laura Ann Rau of Columbus, Mr. Douglass Hubbard of Fredericksburg, Mr. John A. Cypher, Jr., of Kingsville, and to the cited libraries, museums, and institutions which provided all of the photographs and portraits I requested. A special "thank you" is due my very talented niece-by-marriage, Mrs. Penny Grissom Bonnot, who designed the attractive book cover. Mrs. Bonnot is a member of the Art Department at Temple High School.

For the past ten years, I have devoted the summer months and most of my spare time to writing this four-volume series. I was encouraged and inspired to stay the course by the steadfast support of a loving family. My late father and my mother, Herbert C. and Lorene Smith Davis, and my brother and sister, Cecil and Shirley Davis Bonnot, deserve much of the credit for a task completed, and I thank them most of all.

Introduction

In Volume IV of this series about legendary Texians, I have reviewed the lives of a colorful revolutionary leader with a grotesque affliction, a famed Texas Ranger colonel and Indian fighter, an Irish frontiersman whose vision and courage created a ranching empire, and a genuine hero who rivaled Sam Houston in service to Texas. The reader will find that each chapter retains the theme of the series: that the drama of Texas has been played out by a marvelous cast of characters.

Robert McAlpin Williamson limped his way to a special niche in Texas history. Numerous legends cling to this handsome, colorful character. "Three-Legged Willie" overcame a grievous physical handicap to fight at Gonzales and San Jacinto and to serve as first major of the Texas Rangers. This polished aristocrat was also a gifted singer, banjo player, and clown. As an orator and leader of the War Party, he did much to bring on the Texas Revolution. After his famous fighting speech at San Felipe, Mexican General Cos declared Willie the third most-wanted man in Texas. A contemporary described him as a Patrick Henry in the councils and a Solomon on the bench. Robert was to win fame as a brilliant trial lawyer, a courageous district judge, and a politician with a delightfully keen sense of humor. He climaxed a distinguished public career by representing Washington County in both the Texas Congress and the state legislature, then had a county named in his honor. Willie's final years were spent fighting poverty and madness, but he rests today in ground reserved for Texas greats.

The bravery, character, and dedication of Jack Hays defined the nature and image of future Texas Rangers. Absolutely fearless, he became a Ranger captain at age twenty-three by emerging from the group to *prove* his leadership. Blessed with remarkable endurance and an iron constitution, Hays could outfight, outride, and outrun any Comanche. Although his Rangers were typically outnumbered by ten-to-forty to one, they never lost a battle with Indians. This slim, smooth-faced, boyish-looking leader fought a harsh, relentless campaign that terrorized the native population during the Mexican War. Shy, modest, and unassuming, Jack's plain dress and ordinary manner masked his military rank and prowess. As a surveyor-soldier, Hays was the chief protector of the Texas frontier before moving on to tame San Francisco County and build Oakland. Heroic service to Texas brought him national fame, while California afforded Jack opportunity for riches and social prominence.

Richard King made his first fortune in steamboating. Beginning as a stowaway cabin boy, he eventually teamed with Mifflin Kenedy to create a steamboat monopoly on the Rio Grande. Richard used his river seed money to pursue a dream, building a ranch in the dangerous, empty wilderness between the Nueces River and the Rio Grande — the "Wild Horse Desert," where the original Mexican owners dared not live. Captain King's first land purchase, a fortified cow camp on Santa Gertrudis Creek, evolved into the most famous ranch in America. Following the advice of Robert E. Lee to "buy land, and never sell," King came to own 614,000 acres of ranch land. The unique tradition of Los Kineños (the King's men) is rooted in Richard's decision to import an entire Mexican village as his first work force. During the Civil War he went underground as a Confederate quartermaster's agent and funneled Southern cotton to the Mexican neutral port of Bagdad. The end of the war brought a new threat to his budding ranching empire, a decade-long battle with Mexican cattle thieves. During the era of the trail drives to Kansas, King proved to be an innovative businessman by making his herd bosses profit-sharing partners. This rowdy Irishman loved

"Rose Bud" whiskey and bare knuckle fights, but his passions were kept in check by a godly wife. When the famed cattle baron died, management of the King Ranch was passed on to his son-in-law and a succession of Klebergs.

Sul Ross embodies the Southern ideal of the knightly gentleman. He was a fearless but modest warrior, a devoted husband and father, a learned, cultured man who quoted Byron and Shakespeare, and a public figure of spotless integrity. While Sul was a student at Old Baylor at Independence, President Burleson recognized the potential of this rough, combative youth and predicted he would someday be governor of Texas. Only Sam Houston was of greater service to Texas. Ross was, in turn, a Texas Ranger captain, Confederate brigadier general, county sheriff, drafter of the Texas Constitution of 1876, state senator, two-term governor of Texas, and president of Texas A&M College. After winning enduring fame as the Ranger who rescued Cynthia Ann Parker, Sul earned more accolades as a scout and raider in fighting 135 Civil War engagements. As sheriff of McLennan County, he cleaned out the notorious de la Vega grant and was known as the "Model Sheriff of Texas." As governor of Texas, he put his personal prestige on the line to defuse a dangerous, tense situation and help bring an end to the Jaybird-Woodpecker War in Fort Bend County. While he served as president of Texas A&M, Ross was the role model for the cadet corps, who loved this awesome, living legend in their midst.

Writing this series about legendary Texians has been a rewarding experience for me. As I delved into the lives and exploits of thirty-one individuals and families, I discovered a treasure-trove of remarkable, fascinating figures. These early Texians were a special breed of rugged individualists who took on, tamed, and shaped a hostile frontier environment. They rose to the occasion during hard, critical times, and their spunk and grit are the taproot of a colorful, dramatic state heritage. I will, of course, take full responsibility for any errors made in telling of their achievements.

It has been said that Texas is both a state and a state of mind. These books have been my tribute to the molders of this mystique. As a fifth-generation Texan, I trust that the love, pride, and respect I feel for my roots will be sensed and shared by the reader.

I

"Three-Legged Willie" Williamson: A Legend in His Own Time

Historian Henderson Yoakum observed that no other man did more to bring on the Texas Revolution than Robert McAlpin Williamson; indeed, he was the chief orator and propagandist for independence. This handsome minstrel counted William Barret Travis, another dandy and social blade, among his best friends. Robert was equally in character as a refined, poised aristocrat or a salty, colorful humorist. Despite a severe physical handicap, "Three-Legged Willie" was the first major of the Texas Rangers and a cavalry veteran of San Jacinto. He went on to earn a legendary reputation as a great trial lawyer and courageous district judge. When he retired from the Texas political scene, Williamson County was created to honor him in 1848. After a glorious life, Willie spent his last years fighting poverty and insanity and died the ward of his father-in-law.

Bob's grandfather, Micajah Williamson, was of Irish and English stock, a lieutenant colonel in the Continental Army, and the founding father of the Georgia Williamsons. Willie's dad, Peter B., was a soldier, farmer, lawyer, judge, legislator, and Methodist lay preacher. Peter and his first wife, Ann McAlpin, had three children; the youngest, Robert, was born in Clark County, Georgia, in 1804. When Mrs. Williamson died shortly thereafter, her carefree husband was off to Alabama and four other marriages, leaving the three infants with Georgia relatives. Robert was raised by his wealthy grandmother, Sarah Hudson, a member of the social elite in Milledgeville, the new state capital.

After being schooled in Latin, literature, and mathematics, Bob's formal training ended at age fifteen when he was stricken by "white swelling," most likely infantile paralysis, and was bedridden for months. The dread malady left him crippled for life with a useless right leg drawn back at the knee. The limping Willie was forced to use a wooden leg fastened to his knee cap, carry a cane, and tailor his trousers for three legs with a shoe on the protruding right foot. As a Texas contemporary, Noah Smithwick, so aptly put it, "nature had indeed been lavish of her mental gifts" to Bob before "afflicting him with a grievous physical burden."

In 1824 Williamson was admitted to the bar in Milledgeville and soon established a large and lucrative law practice. Legend has it that he abruptly left the state after his ardor for a Georgia belle led Robert to kill a rival suitor in a duel, only to see his love marry another. Disgusted by the whole affair, he left Milledgeville in late November 1825. After visiting his father and practicing some law in Alabama, Willie and a friend, William Sparks, left for New Orleans in 1826. Evidently, he also spent several weeks in Nacogdoches using an assumed name before traveling on to Tennessee and Arkansas, where Samuel Bridge of Hempstead gave him a letter of introduction to Stephen F. Austin. His application for land in Texas shows that Robert arrived at Austin's colony capital, San Felipe de Austin, on June 19, 1827.

The village was located on the west bank of the Brazos River at the lower Atascosito Road Crossing and was entered from the east by ferry. The site was chosen by Austin and Baron de Bastrop in 1823 and laid out in the

2

Mexican style with four plazas or squares. Boasting a population of 200, the town had twenty-five to thirty log cabins and one frame building, the saloon and billiard hall of Cooper and Cheeves. San Felipe was strung out along both sides of the road for half a mile and described by Smithwick as "pretty good as to length, but rather thin." Austin's home on the far end of town was on the west bank of Palmito Creek.

During much of the eight years that Williamson lived at San Felipe, he stayed at Jonathan C. Peyton's small hotel and tavern. Among his early best friends was the hot-tempered Francis W. Johnson, who was clerking in the store of Walter White in 1827 before turning to surveying two years later.[1]

When Willie arrived on the scene at San Felipe in 1827, local society was decidedly masculine with a real scarcity of single ladies. The leader of the "young society" was the lovely widow Mrs. Jane Long, who was described by J. C. Clopper as having a beautiful figure, sparkling

---

[1] Francis White Johnson came to Texas from Tennessee in 1826 to recover from malaria. He became one of the first surveyors in Texas and plotted much of the Ayish District in the late 1820s. In 1831 Frank was elected *alcalde* (mayor) of San Felipe de Austin and was soon a leader in the revolutionary movement. He was a captain in the Anahuac Insurrection of 1832 and joined the Texas army in 1835, becoming inspector general and a close associate of Travis and Bowie. Johnson commanded the Matamoros Expedition in February 1836 and narrowly escaped capture and execution by Mexican general José Urrea. After the war, Frank was in the land business in Austin and Round Rock and spent over thirty years gathering materials for a history of Texas. He died in Mexico on April 8, 1884, while doing research for his book.

In 1914 his manuscript and notes were published by the American Historical Society in an edited, five-volume work, Johnson's *A History of Texas and Texans, by . . . a Leader in the Texas Revolution.* The work included several hundred biographies of early and prominent Texans and was literally fifty years in the making. The most valuable portion of the book was written by Colonel Johnson and contains his personal observations on events in Texas in the 1820s and 1830s. Volume I includes Johnson's manuscript, which was edited into twenty-four chapters by Eugene C. Barker.

3

eyes, and a lively spirit. After she moved to her league of land in the vicinity of Fort Bend in 1828, Noah Smithwick lamented that there were no San Felipe balls or parties for mixed company between then and 1831. Robert quickly made friends with Godwin B. Cotten, a huge, genial old bachelor and editor who started the *Cotton Plant* in 1829. The two amused themselves by holding stag parties with host Cotten calling the merry bouts "love feasts." The bottle passed freely at these sumptuous suppers, and each guest was expected to entertain according to his ability, whether singing, storytelling, or dancing. As Smithwick remembered it,

> ... Judge Williamson was one of the leading spirits on these occasions. Having a natural bent toward the stage, Willie was equally at home conducting a revival meeting or a minstrel show. In the latter performance his wooden leg played an important part, said member being utilized to beat time to his singing.

In addition to being an expert banjo picker, Rob could also entrance listeners as he sang Negro spirituals and hymns.

In such a raucous frontier setting, it is not surprising that most men were tagged with disrespectful nicknames; inevitably, Robert was called "Three-Legged Willie." This broad-shouldered newcomer with deep, blue eyes and black, wavy hair was considered as handsome as Lord Byron, the renowned English poet; both were crippled and loved melancholy and poetic reflections on death. When he first came to San Felipe, Willie wore a coonskin cap and buckskin garb, only to become a fashion plate after prospering in his law practice.

The San Felipe countryside teemed with a wide variety of wild game, and hunting was one of Willie's favorite diversions. Smithwick said Williamson was "a nimrod of no mean order" and recorded one of the most persistent legends about the man. According to Noah, the unarmed Willie once came upon a lost buffalo calf on the prairie. After dismounting he tried to slip a rope over its head,

4

only to have the critter turn on him and charge, butting Robert in the stomach and decking him. When he struggled to his feet, the calf bowled him over again and meandered away. His dander up, Willie responded to this challenge by unbuckling his heavy wooden stirrup strap and giving chase as well as a limping man could. When he caught up with his adversary, he downed the calf with a vicious blow to the head, then bludgeoned it to death. Although his wooden leg was broken in the encounter, the fractured limb was braced up good as new by blacksmith Noah, and "the Judge went on his way rejoicing."

In addition to practicing law in the *alcalde's* court and real estate transactions, Robert became the assistant to Godwin Cotten, editor of the *Texas Gazette,* in late 1829. Each edition of this three-columned newspaper ran four pages; subscription rates were six dollars per year in cash or produce. From January 23 to May 8, 1830, Willie took over the editorship while Cotten became printer and publisher. During this period Williamson deferred to Austin, giving him free reign to write major editorials aimed at placating the Mexican government. Robert wrote the light, amusing editorials and reproduced comical articles found in other newspapers and books.

In the issue of February 6, 1830, he lifted an article titled "A Life Saved by Brandy" from a New York paper. The piece told of a headwaiter returning to his frigid room with a kettle of burning charcoal to ward off the cold. When the room temperature became too comfortable, the waiter dozed off and was near suffocation when a boarder thirsting for brandy barged into his room wanting the key to the liquor cellar. The intruder applied himself to the prone waiter and managed to revive him after a herculean effort. To the writer of the article, it seemed obvious that the waiter would surely have died if both boarders had belonged to a temperance union. This observer concluded, "We therefore pass this life perserved to the credit of spirituous liquor, which deducted from the

30,000 annually lost from the same cause, leaves a balance of 29,999."

Always on the lookout for the amusing, Bob was delighted to find a society notice from Salem, Massachusetts, announcing the marriage of Mr. Lewis Plum of Newark and Miss Elizabeth Lemon of Salem. The notice concluded with the wry commentary, "This is certainly a fruitful match, but we hope none of the little plums will inherit their mother's acidity." Another method of entertaining his readers was the publishing of good hunting stories, with Willie's favorite being the tall tale about the voracious nature of the "Turkey Buzzard."

Editing the paper must have been fun to Williamson, but he abruptly left the staff in May 1830, probably because Cotten could not pay his salary. Seven months later Bob took the paper back as editor and changed its name to the *Mexican Citizen* in 1831. His new partner was John Aitken, a veteran newspaperman from Pensacola, Florida, but the *Citizen* ceased publication that December; the press was eventually moved to Brazoria and used to print the *Texas Republican.*

Although the Mexican State Colonization Law of 1830 prohibited further immigration from the United States, Article 10 of that statute provided that "no change shall be made with respect to colonies already established." Stephen F. Austin interpreted this restriction as not binding on either his colony or that of Green De Witt. His total faith and trust in Willie was revealed when Austin ordered his secretary, Samuel May Williams, to give Robert all the signed land certificate blanks he wanted. These valuable documents were for those immigrants en route and were as good as passports into Texas.

In 1831 Williamson became the agent for Ben Milam's colony and introduced William Barret Travis for a land grant upon his arrival from Alabama that May. It seems that he and Travis were kindred spirits, and they quickly became the best of friends while boarding at Jonathan Pey-

6

ton's hotel. The hotel was also a home, and Mrs. Peyton operated a two-table boardinghouse; the plain fare was set out on the men's table while the more tasty dishes were put on *her* table to be shared with other ladies. Such culinary discrimination inspired the two pals to play a prank on their hostess. While Willie occupied Mrs. Peyton with a steady stream of flattery, Travis exchanged the provisions on the tables and, at least for once, the menfolk enjoyed the finer fare. Due to the surplus of lawyers in town, Travis and another young attorney, Patrick Jack, moved to Anahuac in the summer of 1831.

Anahuac was located on a bluff near the point where the Trinity River empties into Galveston Bay and was the major port of entry for East Texas at the time. The settlement became a focal point of friction after the Colonization Law of 1830 placed high tariffs on United States imports and provided for sending customs collectors to all gulf ports. A Kentucky bully named John Davis Bradburn was given command of the Mexican garrison of convict-soldiers at Anahuac. Bradburn had left Kentucky after a jailbreak involving a slave dispute and had gone to Mexico, where he joined the army as an officer and rose to the rank of colonel.

A showdown was triggered when Buck Travis played a practical joke on Juan Bradburn and was arrested for the "crime" of making Juan look silly in Anglo eyes. After Bradburn refused to return three runaway slaves to their owner, William Logan of Opelousas, Louisiana, Buck was hired to assist Logan in claiming his property, only to be told that the slaves had joined the Mexican army. One night a tall stranger calling himself "Billew" gave a Mexican sentry a letter warning that a hundred armed men were at the Sabine River and intended to forceably recover the slaves. The alarmed Juan called out the garrison in the dead of night, but a week passed with no invasion. Suspecting Travis of the prank, Bradburn ordered that he and Patrick Jack be arrested but made no formal charges against them. After building two brick kilns to serve as their jail, he announced plans to hold a military trial at Matamoros.

In May 1832, Williamson received letters from James Lindsay and Monroe Edwards telling him that his friends, Jack and Travis, had been arrested at Anahuac. Willie hurriedly raised a company of forty volunteers and marched to their relief, only to find that Bradburn had already put the two on a schooner. He immediately confronted Juan, pounded his fists, and shouted:

> Dr. Labadie and I are determined that Jack shall have his liberty. I tell you, sir, Jack must come on shore or you or I will be a dead man by tomorrow. I tell you, Colonel, that all hell will not stop me . . . There are many more besides us to make my words good. Blood will flow if Jack is not released by tomorrow.

Cowed by this brash warning, Bradburn ordered his prisoners brought ashore and released, prompting Williamson and his men to give "three hearty cheers" before returning to San Felipe. As soon as they departed, however, Juan again arrested Jack and Travis along with James Lindsay.

Upon hearing of this treachery, Robert was chosen to recruit a new force at San Felipe on June 4, 1832. In writing to the men of Brazoria, he appealed to them to "turn out strong" and join his men at Lynch's ferry on the San Jacinto River. Some sixty of Austin's colonists assembled a few miles below Liberty and elected Willie's friend, Francis Johnson, as their captain. When an agreement to exchange prisoners was repudiated by Bradburn, the Texians retreated to Turtle Bayou, six miles from Anahuac, to await the arrival of a cannon from Brazoria. While camped there on June 13, they adopted the Turtle Bayou Resolutions, a series of four declarations drafted by Williamson and six others, to be sent to Col. José Mexia of Santa Anna's army. One of the resolutions read as follows:

> Resolved: That as freemen devoted to a correct inter-

pretation, and enforcement of the Constitution, and laws, according to their true Spirit — We pledge our lives and fortunes in support of the same, and of the distinguished leader [Santa Anna], who is now so gallantly fighting in defence of Civil liberty.

Soon after Col. José de las Piedras brought Mexican troops from Nacogdoches and arranged a conference with the Texians, news reached Anahuac that Capt. John T. Austin had defeated the Mexican garrison at Velasco. The tense situation was defused on July 3 when Piedras agreed to release Jack and Travis to Johnson and to relieve Bradburn of his command. The Mexican troops at Anahuac declared for Santa Anna and sailed away to join him while the victorious Texians returned to their homes. By this time, Williamson's actions had made him an acknowledged leader of the war party, and he had publicly broken with Stephen F. Austin. In fact, he told a friend, "We must raise that fellow off the land if he don't come to."

Robert played a key role in the Convention of 1833, which met at San Felipe on April 1. This gathering of some fifty delegates was opposed by Austin, who thought that Bexar (San Antonio) leaders should take the lead in pushing for political reforms. William H. Wharton, a hothead leader of the war party, was chosen president of the convention, which resolved that Texas should be split from Coahuila and granted separate statehood within the Mexican federal system. Willie served on a committee chaired by Sam Houston which drafted a proposed state constitution for Texas, a document that was Anglo-American in every important detail. Austin was chosen to present these demands to the Mexican government, a mission that would lead to his imprisonment.

In the fall of 1833, Willie announced as a candidate for the office of *alcalde* of the San Felipe district, a position combining the functions of a mayor and city judge. Although he had a flourishing law practice, Austin's lament that the non-paying position was "seldom sought by those best qualified to fill it" appealed to his sense of civic duty. Fellow attorney Travis took time out from his own busy practice to "labor mightily" for his friend, going so far as to bet a hat and ten dollars on the outcome. By this time the two cronies were borrowing small sums from each other, and Willie frequently engaged Buck as an assistant in major cases.

Even though his only opponent, Silas Dinsmore, carried San Felipe by thirty votes, Williamson won all the rural boxes in the December election and was installed in office on January 1, 1834. On February 5 he appointed Travis to a one-year term as secretary of the *ayuntamiento* (governing council) at San Felipe. In this capacity he took care of all official correspondence and could speak out but not vote. The two had a similar attitude toward Mexican officialdom. Both simply went through the motions in carrying out — or even brushing off — directives sent by Ramón Musquiz, the political chief at San Antonio, while they vigorously asserted themselves in protecting the interests of the local district.

In April 1834, Willie accompanied Buck to a court hosted by Dr. Pleasant W. Rose near Stafford's Point. Travis was there to defend Mr. "M," who had been accused by his neighbor, Mr. "A," of stealing and marking his unbranded calf. The court assembled under a liveoak tree, with David G. Burnet as presiding judge. In addition to Williamson, other lawyers present were Patrick and William Jack. Area families came to socialize and watch the show, and Ben Fort Smith donated two barbecued calves to feed the crowd. During the trial the men slept in the Rose girls' playhouse. Although Mr. M was quickly found guilty by the jury — all could see the calf with his brand sucking a cow with Mr. A's brand — there remained a sticky problem: a guilty verdict would send Mr. M to a Mexican jail. While the court and assembled spectators recessed for a sumptuous barbecue dinner, Mr. Smith quietly drew Mr. A aside and bought the cow *and* calf. The new owner requested that charges against Mr. M be dropped, the court agreed, and the case was thus settled. Once the tension was resolved, Mrs. Rose asked to hear some scripture reading and preaching but, alas, no one had a Bible. All was not lost: a Mr. Woodruff volunteered to lead in prayer before Willie led in the singing of "On Jordan's Stormy Banks" and "Come, Thou Fount of Every Blessing." The thoughtful Travis later sent the Rose girls two small books but could not find a Bible in San Felipe for their mother.

News of Austin's imprisonment in Mexico City reached San Felipe on February 1, 1834. The previous October he had written an angry, indiscreet letter to the *ayuntamiento* at San Antonio suggesting that they go ahead "without a moment's delay" in organizing a separate state government for Texas even without official Mexican approval, a recommendation he said was "the only means of saving us from anarchy and ruin." Once this letter became known, Austin was arrested at Saltillo while en route to Texas.

On April 28, 1834, Williamson and Travis wrote a strong petition to the Mexican Congress requesting Austin's release from prison. This resolution from San Felipe was followed by similar appeals for Austin's freedom from Matagorda, Liberty, Bastrop, Gonzales, and Brazoria. All of these petitions were designed to shift responsibility for his mission to those representatives who attended the Convention of 1833. Since he had opposed that gathering, his actions were simply those of an able spokesman and were not his own opinions. The Williamson-Travis petition noted that Austin's fateful letter represented not his views but those of a large majority "of forty thousand citizens, zealous of their requests and suspicious of him." The resolution went on to state:

> If any wrong has been committed, it has not been by Colonel Austin — If any treason has been intended the whole people of Texas alone are guilty. He represented in his letter their feelings and intentions at the time he was dispatched to Mexico; and if he erred or violated any law, or was wanting in proper respect, or attach-

ment to the government, the people of Texas should alone be the sufferers . . .

To the two Texian lawyers, his release would

> furnish to the people of Texas renewed evidence that the reign of despotism had ceased, and that all their just and reasonable requests will receive considerate attention from the ruling authorities of the country.

All of these petitions, however, had negligible effect on the Mexican government, and Austin was to spend eighteen months in prison or under house arrest.

In March 1834, the state legislature of Coahuila-Texas created the Department of the Brazos to be headed by a political chief, a rank higher than that of *alcalde*. Governor Augustín Viesca asked that the San Felipe *ayuntamiento* submit three nominees for his consideration. The appointed chief would serve until the general election of May 1835. After Williamson, Travis, and J. H. C. Miller were suggested for the post, Buck informed Political Chief Musquiz that Miller was ineligible for the office since he was not a colonist or naturalized citizen. Since Governor Viesca had less-than-fond memories of Willie and Buck's role at Anahuac, he chose to disregard the nominees and instead chose Henry Smith of Brazoria as political chief, even though he did not live at the seat of government, San Felipe, and would thus be absent much of the time. By the fall of 1834, both Robert and Travis were pressuring Smith to call a convention to push for separate statehood. On September 11, Williamson wrote Smith from San Antonio, saying he had lost all hope that Santa Anna would implement his professed liberal policies and calling the Mexican general "a military despot . . . whose ignorance is alone equaled by his arrogance."

By this time, war clouds were forming on the Texas horizon. After dissolving the Mexican Congress and disbanding state legislatures, General Santa Anna suspended the federal constitution in October 1835, becoming in effect a military dictator. In January he had sent

Capt. Antonio Tenorio and a small detachment of Mexican troops to reestablish the customshouse at Anahuac and stop the rich smuggling trade. On June 10, 1835, Andrew Briscoe, a prominent merchant, was arrested for allegedly violating a tariff law. The news reached San Felipe just as word arrived that Santa Anna had suspended all civil government in Coahuila-Texas. On June 22 a secret meeting of the war party at San Felipe authorized the fiery Travis "to collect a force and expel the garrison at Anahuac."

The next day, Robert presided over a meeting of some of the oldest and most respected colonists, a gathering of conservatives, not hotheads, that denounced Santa Anna for violating the Constitution of 1824. While Willie was busy drafting a famous address, Travis and twenty-five men appeared at Anahuac on June 27 and demanded that Tenorio surrender his post; the next morning the Mexican officer gave up without firing a shot and promised to lead his troops from Texas.

The stage was now set for one of Williamson's most outstanding acts — a famous, fighting speech at San Felipe on July 4, 1835, in which he bluntly labeled Santa Anna a dictator and a sworn enemy of republicanism. Robert suggested the immediate, forceful seizure of San Antonio and admonished his fellow citizens:

> ... Let us no longer sleep in our posts; let us resolve to prepare for War — and resolve to defend our country against the danger that threatens it — A sacrifice has to be made ... already we can almost hear the bugles of our enemies — already have some of them landed on our coast and you must prepare to fight. Liberty or Death should be our determination and let us one and all unite to protect our country from all invasion — and not lay down our arms so long as a soldier is seen in our limits ...

On August 1, Gen. Martín Perfecto de Cos, the brother-in-law of Santa Anna and newly appointed military commandant of Texas, ordered the arrest of eight

Texians; they were to be turned over or Mexican troops would take them by force. Heading his priority list was the surrender of Lorenzo de Zavala, a liberal former Mexcian governor. Next was "W. B. Travis, esq, and next Robt. M. Williamson."

Shortly after his July 4 speech, Willie led one of three San Felipe companies sent to the relief of Robert Coleman's troops at Parker's Fort near present Groesbeck. Coleman's men had been surrounded by Tehuacana Indians, who were defeated by the San Felipe reinforcements at Tehuacana Springs and pursued up the Trinity to near present Dallas. After taking part in this expedition, fugitive Williamson moved to Mina (Bastrop) for his own safety. There he was elected a delegate to the Consultation scheduled to meet at San Felipe on October 16, 1835. Before that gathering, however, he answered an appeal for reinforcements from Gonzales, where eighteen Texians had refused to turn over a six-pound cannon to 180 Mexican cavalrymen sent from San Antonio. Captain Williamson led a Mina company of mounted riflemen and took part in the Battle of Gonzales on October 2. In fact, it was either he or Col. John H. Moore who suggested the phrase "Come and Take It," which was sewn on the Gonzales battle flag.

After receiving an honorable discharge signed by Colonel Moore, Willie used his speaking and writing abilities to recruit and obtain supplies for Stephen F. Austin's Texian army, which was gathering at Gonzales. This force started for San Antonio on October 12 and besieged the city on the twenty-fourth.

Since many of the delegates elected to the Consultation were in the army, there was no quorum at San Felipe until November 3, 1835. Among the able delegates answering the first roll call were Sam Houston from Nacogdoches, John A. Wharton from Columbia, Wylie Martin from San Felipe, and Lorenzo de Zavala from Harrisburg. After Dr. Branch T. Archer was chosen president of the Consultation, a committee of twelve (one from each

14

district) was selected to draft a statement of the official view of the gathering. Willie represented Mina on this committee with Wharton, another member of the war party, as chairman. Although both favored outright independence, a Sam Houston motion to establish a provisional state government based on the Constitution of 1824 passed by a vote of 33–14. Robert then proposed one of four plans to the Wharton committee, a draft characterized as "the blunt statement of a man who tried to tone down the expression of his real feelings to meet the wishes of a squeamish majority." The Williamson document declared Texas independent of the existing Mexican government without declaring for any other form of Mexican government. Of the eight articles included in the Wharton committee report of November 7, three were taken from Robert's drafts.

When Colonel Austin had the opportunity to read this report as adopted by the convention, he observed that it tended as much toward independence as to adherence to the Constitution of 1824. Due to Willie's determined efforts, the final declaration satisfied the war party and had "a brusquer tone" than their numerical strength warranted. On November 18, Williamson received a "Dear Willy" letter from his friend, Francis Johnson, who was serving under Austin during the Siege of Bexar. The appeal read in part:

> For God's sake have the battering piece forwarded with ball, etc. Tent cloth and other things are in great requisition, and it is the only thing that will keep the present force together.

Rob turned this request over to the General Council placed in charge of governmental affairs.

After voting to form a provisional state government, the Consultation elected Henry Smith of Brazoria as provisional governor to serve with a General Council of twelve, one from each district. On November 28, 1835, the council chose Williamson over James Kerr as first major of the Texas Rangers. The corps was to be divided into three companies of fifty-six men each; a captain was to head each company, but he would not be elected by his men. Each Ranger would be paid $1.25 per day and had to furnish his own food, clothing, horses, ammunition, and supplies. As major of the Rangers, Robert was subject to the orders of Sam Houston, the commander-in-chief of the Texas army. The Rangers were an adjunct to the army, with the primary task of protecting the colonists from the Indians.

On February 14, 1836, the General Council ordered Williamson "to fortify strategic points as to more surely protect the frontier from Indian attacks." While visiting at San Felipe on February 17, Robert met Col. William Fairfax Gray, a Virginia speculator who was trying to arrange a loan to the Texas government. In his diary Colonel Gray described Willie as "an intrepid Indian fighter"; however, the colonel turned down an offer of half a league of land in Milam's colony for his good horse because Gray didn't know what "confidence" to put in Robert or his titles.

It was during this period that Williamson had his most satisfactory scrap with Indians. After he and five Rangers were trailed by some savages intent on stealing their horses, he decided to try a ruse. Knowing that Indians tended to attack a camp just before dawn, the Rangers built a large campfire, wrapped their blankets around man-sized logs, and hid in the brush. Just at the expected time, the warriors stealthily approached and plunged their knives into the dummies; as they straightened up they were all mowed down by Ranger rifle fire.

While Robert was on patrol and camped at Gonzales, news reached him that his pal, William Barret Travis, was surrounded by Santa Anna's Mexican army at the Alamo. Since he was under orders to guard the frontier, Willie could do no more than issue a proclamation to his "Fellow Citizens of Texas," urging that they go to Buck's relief. He did all he could to help, telling area residents that "we are drying beef for them; we are hunting and also grinding corn." When General Houston arrived at Gonzales on March 11, 1836, he sent Williamson to Bastrop to assemble all Ranger forces and take personal command there. His orders called for Willie's men to protect the frontier settlers in their retreat and to serve as scouts and spies for the Texas army.

When news of the fall of the Alamo reached Bastrop, the calm and unruffled Williamson helped evacuate the town and reassured the panic-stricken civilians as they packed their belongings. One of the refugees, John H. Jenkins, Sr., later recalled a special favor from the Ranger major: his own shoes were worn out, so Robert gave him a pair of good boots which were "indeed acceptable." Bastrop was soon deserted, and Willie's Rangers sank all the boats near town and camped on the opposite bank of the Colorado. When a Mexican army of 600 occupied the empty town a few days later, Robert and his small detail beat a hasty retreat.

After Willie's Rangers reached Cole's Settlement (later Independence), he received word that Fannin and his army had been massacred at Goliad. He posted notice of the disaster for refugees, warning them to move fast. By this time General Houston's Texas army had fallen back from the Colorado rather than fight General Sesma's Mexican force camped on the opposite bank. On March 31, Houston's troops camped on the west bank of the Brazos opposite Groce's Landing. It was there that Major Williamson finally made contact with the commander-in-chief. In covering the flight of the settlers exposed by Houston's retreat, Ranger Noah Smithwick described the desolation as follows:

> Houses were standing open, the beds unmade, the breakfast things still on the table, pans of milk moulding in the dairies. There were cribs full of corn, smoke houses full of bacon, yards full of chickens that ran after us for food, nests of eggs in every fence corner, young corn and garden truck rejoicing in the rain, cattle cropping the luxuriant grass, hogs, fat

17

and lazy, wallowing in the mud, all abandoned . . .
Wagons were so scarce that it was impossible to remove household goods; many of the women and children even had to walk.

There were broken down wagons and household
goods scattered all along the road. Stores with quite
valuable stocks of goods stood open, the goods on the
shelves, no attempt having been made to remove them.

Robert's frustration with the chaotic situation is revealed in two letters he wrote General Houston from
Washington-on-the Brazos on April 7. In the first note he
told of enlisting recruits for the army and sending out spy
patrols; in a follow-up letter, the Ranger leader bluntly
demanded a written request for a visit with his superior.

Shortly after the Texas army crossed the swollen
Brazos on the *Yellowstone* on April 13, Willie and his
men finally joined the main force. When they reached
Robert's farm and a major crossroads, the "Which-Way
Tree," eight miles east of present Tomball, the army
turned right on a forced march headed for Harrisburg
and a certain battle with General Santa Anna. According
to Dr. Labadie, a member of Houston's medical staff, Williamson came galloping up to Sam some six miles down
the road and was ordered to find the Redland Company
and tell them to join the army "as it had now changed its
course to Harrisburg." At 3:30 P.M. on April 21, 1836,
General Houston formed his infantry into two columns
about a thousand yards across, with the Texian cavalry
on the extreme right. This unit of sixty horsemen included Willie, a member of William H. Smith's cavalry
company, and was commanded by his Georgia cousin,
Mirabeau B. Lamar, who had been promoted from private to colonel the day before. It seems that Smithwick
and the main body of the Ranger force missed the Battle
of San Jacinto, an eighteen-minute total rout of Santa
Anna's Mexican army. (Williamson later received 640
acres of donation land for having fought at San Jacinto.)

On December 22, 1836, the First Congress of the

Republic of Texas divided Texas into four judicial districts and elected Robert as judge of the Third Judicial District. As such, he was also an associate justice of the supreme court, but that body seldom convened during his term of office.

As one who had helped to *make* Texas law, Williamson was qualified by training and experience to be a district judge. He was to hold office for four years and receive a salary of $3,000 per year. Willie's Third District included Austin, Washington, Milam, Mina, Colorado, and Gonzales counties. Two annual sessions of the court were to begin in March and September in each county of the district, with each session limited to six days.

Being a circuit district judge was an arduous task. Since courthouses were few and far between, Robert often presided in log cabins. All the buildings in Columbus had been burned by General Houston's retreating army, so Willie convened the first district court session ever held in Colorado County under a century-old live oak in April 1837. People often ignored summons to district court duty, and Judge Williamson fined such recalcitrant jurors twenty dollars. Regular sessions of the court were often delayed due to bad weather or travel hardships. During court sessions, lawyers traveled and camped out with the judge and were entertained by Willie's campfire singing, banjo-playing, and storytelling; in fact, his droll tales and anecdotes about him made Robert one of the most renowned men in Texas.

Williamson was among the most humane judges of his day, and he tended to assess sentences as light as the law allowed.[2] He could be selective in his judgments, however,

---

[2] In another early case tried in Columbus by Judge James W. Robinson, the hapless W. H. Bibbs was found guilty of grand larceny (probably cattle theft) and threw himself upon the mercy of the court. Judge Robinson decreed that the prisoner should receive thirty-nine lashes on his bare back, be branded on the right hand with the letter "T" (for thief), and pay the cost of suit or remain in custody. Once the judge was informed that the sum of $500 could not be found west of

and numerous tales attest to his tough, no-nonsense approach. The following Williamson tale appeared in the Huntsville *Texas Banner* on July 22, 1849. It seems that Willie was about to pronounce the death penalty on a man found guilty of murder by the jury. When the condemned man was asked if he had anything to say, the shaking, ashen-faced prisoner was so overcome by fear that he lost his voice. At this point the judge said, "Mr. Sheriff, I think you had better take him out and hang him. He has lost all consciousness and sensibility, and his neck can be broken without his knowing it, or feeling it."

On another occasion, Robert concluded a murder trial by sentencing the guilty party to be hanged that very day. Shocked by such an action, the lawyers, jury, and local residents drafted a hasty petition, praying that more time be granted the condemned man. Unmoved, Judge Williamson replied that the man had been found guilty, and that the jail was too unsafe and uncomfortable for anyone to stay there longer than necessary. The man was hanged.

Even lawyers had to watch their step in the judge's court. Once an attorney named Charlton stated a point of law, but Willie refused to admit the statement as sufficient proof and replied, "Your law, Sir, give us the book and page, Sir." Pulling out his pistol, the frustrated lawyer retorted, "This is my law, Sir, and this, Sir, is my book," drawing out a Bowie knife. Pointing his pistol toward the court, he concluded, "And this is the page." The unruffled judge responded, "Your law is not good, Sir; the proper authority is *Colt on revolvers!*" When Williamson trained his five-shooter on his adversary's head, the chastised attorney dodged the point of the argument and turned to the jury to try a new — and safer — legal approach.

The primitive nature of the jails that Robert encountered was attested to by Dr. Ashbel Smith, foreman of the

---

the Colorado, he remitted that portion of the sentence, and the bloodied, scarred culprit was released from custody.

Harrisburg County grand jury during the spring 1839 term of the court. The county jail contained two tiny, crowded cells separated by a narrow "ante-room" for women. Writing in the June 5 issue of the *Telegraph and Texas Register,* Dr. Smith graphically denounced the jail:

> ... The effluvia now environing the jail for some feet around are so potent as to sicken the stoutest stomach ...
>
> The night tubs of the jail are emptied only once in seven days. During this period their foul and putrifying contents stand in the cells of the prisoners ...

Judge Williamson's nerve and courage were put to the test when he convened the first district court session in newly organized Shelby County in 1837. This border county along the Sabine River had been a part of the old "Neutral Ground" between 1806 and 1819, and had established a well-deserved reputation as a haven for fugitives and outlaws. The night before the court convened, locals held a mass meeting and resolved not to submit to the courts of the Republic of Texas. The next morning, Willie stationed himself behind a dry goods box and announced that the court was in session. Immediately a local thug stepped forward to announce that area residents would not allow a district court session to be held. When Robert mildly asked what legal authority he could give for such a procedure, the spokesman drew a Bowie knife, slammed it on the box, and snarled, "This, sir, is the law of Shelby County!" The undaunted judge whipped out his long-barreled pistol and thundered, "If *that* is the law of Shelby County, *this* is the constitution which overrides all law!" Williamson then turned to the sheriff and ordered him to call the grand jury while the toughie retreated from the courtroom. After this confrontation, Robert's reputation skyrocketed amid rumors that firearms were always at hand during his court sessions.

On Monday, September 4, 1837, Willie's second tour in

the First Judicial District began at Nacogdoches in the "Old Stone Fort." When the court's business was completed, a testimonial from the grand jury to the judge read as follows:

> [The grand jury] cannot surrender . . . the trust with which they have been clothed without bearing ample testimony to the talents, ability, and independence which have characterized his honor Judge R. M. Williamson now presiding in this court; we have listened with great pleasure and profit to his able, learned, and patriotic charge . . . We have admired the independence, honesty and praiseworthy impartiality which have so signally marked his cause.

On behalf of the lawyers who had appeared in court, Gen. Thomas J. Rusk told of his pride in the judicial proceedings in a speech to the grand jury. That December, Robert's court activities concluded for the year with a session of the supreme court in Houston.

On April 21, 1837, he married Mary Jane Edwards, the daughter of Col. Gustavus E. Edwards of Austin County. The colonel was a member of Austin's "Old Three Hundred" colonists, a veteran of the War of 1812, and a man of means. Coming to Texas in 1822, he received a league of land in present Wharton County on August 19, 1824. Initially, he lived on an Austin County farm and owned and operated the Robinson ferry just below old Washington. After Mary Jane's mother died at sea en route from New Orleans to Galveston, Colonel Edwards took his daughter back to Nashville to be educated before she rejoined him in Texas.

Williamson was totally devoted to his new bride, and the couple settled on a farm at Gay Hill between Brenham and Independence in Washington County. Throughout their married life the generosity and kindness of Mary Jane made their residence "the home of the orphan." Sudden wealth came Willie's way on January 14, 1839, when the Texas Congress authorized him to receive ten certificates, each good for a league and labor of land, for his services as the agent of empresario Ben Milam. By this time he and Mary Jane had their first of seven children, Hoxie Collingsworth, with another due soon; of the Williamson offspring, only Julia Rebecca and Willie Annexus lived to maturity and raised families.

In failing health and tired of being away from home, Robert resigned his district judgeship on January 22, 1839, and spent the next two years practicing law. He immediately began to sell some of his large holdings in San Patricio, Aransas, Robertson, and Bexar counties, receiving $9,000 from land sales alone in 1841.

In 1840 Willie was elected to represent Washington County in the Fifth Texas Congress; he was to serve four full terms in the House of Representatives and an abbreviated term in the Senate. As a politician he became known as a conservative, an advocate of economy, and guardian of the public treasury. Perhaps his most noteworthy service came in the Sixth Congress, 1841–42, a time when "mad extravagance ruled the hour and the country seemed on the verge of destruction." After taking his seat on November 6, 1841, Robert was appointed to five key standing committees: the judiciary, post offices, foreign relations and retrenchment, naval affairs, and the state of the republic. On November 19, he was part of a select committee majority which reported that President Lamar's act in ordering the Texas navy to join the naval forces of Yucatan against Mexico was in violation of a "plain legislative mandate." An act of the Fifth Congress had provided that the navy was to be laid up "in ordinary," so the president had clearly violated the law.

In an opening speech advocating the recall of the navy, Williamson accused his cousin Lamar of making a lawless disposition of the small fleet and lambasted the "profligacy" of his administration, contending that "our Treasury had been broken in upon, and its means squandered" when Lamar sent out the Santa Fe Expedition and dispatched the navy to ally with Yucatan. On December 6, Willie supported a joint resolution to recall the navy, although his motion failed that would have struck out the bill's preamble which criticized Lamar personally. After the motion to bring in the navy failed by a vote of 20 to 18, Robert on December 17 voted against appointing a committee that would have drafted articles of impeachment against the president.

On December 4, 1844, Williamson began a brief term as a senator in the Eighth Congress. When the election returns were challenged by Jesse Grimes, the seat was declared vacant on January 4, 1845, and Robert was succeeded by Grimes on January 28. However, the irrepressible Willie was back in the House of Representatives for the ninth and final session of the Republic of Texas Congress. He was such an ardent supporter of annexation by the United States that he named a baby son Willie Annexus when he was born on January 13, 1845.

After Texas became a state in the Union, Rob became a staunch national Democrat and represented Milam and Washington counties as a state senator in both the First and Second Legislature, serving from February 19, 1846, until March 20, 1848, ending his career as a lawmaker. In 1849 the tired, ailing Willie suffered his only political defeat when he was narrowly beaten by Volney E. Howard in a race for the U.S. Congress. He entered the campaign late and was obviously off form; the old fire and fluency of his speech was gone. Howard's margin of victory came in the Rio Grande Valley, where a host of newcomers simply did not know the legendary "Three-Legged Willie." The sickly old warrior-statesman retired to his Gay Hill farm, only to announce for lieutenant governor in 1851. However, the rigors of campaigning led to an early withdrawal from the race due to "considerations of a private nature"; it was rumored that he was drinking too much whiskey, probably to dull the pain of some recurring, unknown illness.

In his prime, Willie's repartee with political opponents made him the subject of countless tales. For example, it seems that he was once opposed by a doctor who tried to embarrass him by charging that Robert had shot two men. The unruffled Williamson broke up, and won over, his rustic audience by retorting:

> On two occasions under the peculiar force of circumstances I have been forced to kill two men. But, my dear doctor, tell us — how many men have *you* killed in the practice of medicine?

At another time Rob was seemingly bested in debate by Col. Benjamin Rush Wallace, an aristocratic Virginian and West Pointer from San Augustine. When he rose to reply, the forlorn-looking Willie groaned out, "Dead, yes, dead, Mr. Speaker, slain by that mighty instrument which in the hands of Samson killed thousands of Philistines." The uproar of laughter which followed drowned out the colonel's shrill shouts for satisfaction.

During Sam Houston's second term as president of the republic, there was talk of temporarily moving supreme court sessions from Washington to Galveston. Williamson reacted to the proposal by ridiculing the island city as an "isolated sandbar inhabited by pelicans, sea gulls and the lordliest sort of damned rascals his two blue eyes had ever gazed on." When his friend, Galveston County Congressman J. W. Jones, was asked if he was going to respond, Jones ruefully admitted, "What would be the use? The next time he would be still worse."

Even in his public prayers, Willie was prone to add a dash of humor and plain talk to the Lord. Old-timers in Wharton recall the story about him praying for rain. It seems that the judge made a business trip to Victoria in the midst of a terrible drought. When he noticed a large group of farmers entering a local church, he decided to join them. The crowd had come to a prayer meeting to seek God's "showers of blessing." Once the moderator noticed Williamson's somber frock coat, he said, "Brother, will you lead us in this prayer for rain?" Willie promptly got down on his knees and said in a deep, commanding voice:

> O Lord, . . . send us a bounteous rain that will cause

the crops to fruit in all their glory and the earth to turn again to that beauteous green that comes from abundant showers. Lord, send us a bounteous one that will make corn ears shake hands across the row and not one of these damn drizzle-drazzle rains that will make nubbins that all hell can't shuck. We want a gulley-washer and a creek flooder — not next week, but now!

Before his retirement from politics, Williamson had sold most of his land grants. His generosity and tendency to let money slip through his hands left him in poverty in his twilight years. Any struggling young attorney could count on free assistance and advice at Willie's law office. In the summer evenings he loved to sit on the front porch of his farm home singing hymns and playing the banjo; he would sing the verse, and his Negro slaves joined in the chorus of such favorites as "Light House."

Robert's ire was aroused after the secret Know-Nothing Party was organized in Texas in 1854. This group was opposed to Catholics or foreign-born persons holding public office and favored stricter naturalization laws and literacy tests for voting. When members were asked to state their platform, their secrecy rule required them to reply, "I know nothing." Senator Houston endorsed their principles in a letter, and the party captured local offices in San Antonio and Galveston in 1854. The next year the Know Nothings held a statewide convention at Washington-on-the-Brazos and nominated David C. Dickson for governor. In the election of 1855, Dickson lost to the incumbent Democratic governor, Elisha M. Pease, by only 4,000 votes. Although his "feeble health" kept him from a statewide campaign against the Know Nothings, Willie did write a long letter from Independence which appeared in the *Texas Ranger* at Washington on July 28, 1855. In this, his last major public declaration, Williamson condemned both the party and Senator Houston.

On November 17, 1856, Robert's beloved helpmate, Mary Jane, died suddenly at Independence, a loss from which her husband never recovered. The next year a renewed attack of illness affected Willie's mind and left him fighting insanity. The children were sent to live with Georgia relatives while their father was rescued by the kind-hearted Colonel Edwards, who had moved to his land in Wharton County in July 1837. The colonel brought his son-in-law to his home in Wharton and for three pathetic and lonely years, the helpless Williamson was cared for by slaves.

After becoming critically ill on November 17, 1859, Robert lingered for three days in feverish delirium, attended by a single faithful old servant. When the merciful end came on November 20, his last words were, "Life sinks beneath the horizon." Willie was buried in Wharton and rested there for almost seventy years; then, in 1930, his body was reinterred in the State Cemetery at Austin. At the same time, a joint session of the legislature honored his memory. In 1936 the Texas Centennial Commission marked the site of his last home on Rusk Street in Wharton. His self-description, which appeared in the *Texas Ranger* on July 28, 1855, is an appropriate epitaph:

> I have lived in Texas near thirty years, and in that time I have rendered all the service in my power, so help me God — and my only regret now is that in the darkest hours I could then do no more for her.

Sketch of William Barret
Travis (by Wiley Martin,
December 1835).
— Courtesy Perry-Castañeda
Library, The University of
Texas at Austin

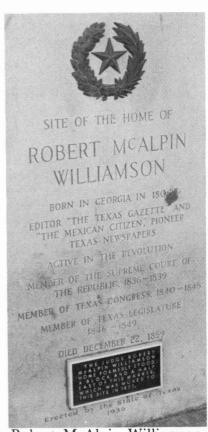

SITE OF THE HOME OF

ROBERT McALPIN
WILLIAMSON

BORN IN GEORGIA IN 1804
EDITOR "THE TEXAS GAZETTE" AND
"THE MEXICAN CITIZEN", PIONEER
TEXAS NEWSPAPERS

ACTIVE IN THE REVOLUTION

MEMBER OF THE SUPREME COURT OF
THE REPUBLIC, 1836–1839
&
MEMBER OF TEXAS CONGRESS, 1840–1845

MEMBER OF TEXAS LEGISLATURE
1846–1849

DIED DECEMBER 22, 1859

Erected by the State of Texas
1930

Robert M. "Three-Legged
Willie" Williamson.
— Courtesy Perry-Castañeda
Library, The University of
Texas at Austin

Robert McAlpin Williamson
State Marker, Courthouse
Square, Wharton, Texas.
— Photo by J. C. Hoke
Wharton, Texas

28

District Court Oak at Columbus (1890s).
— Courtesy Columbus Sesquicentennial Booklet, 1973

District Court Oak at Columbus (1988).
— Photo by J. C. Hoke, Wharton, Texas

II

Jack Hays:
He Fought the Good Fight

John Coffee ("Jack") Hays is considered the greatest Indian fighter in Texas history; the fearsome Comanches called him "Devil Yack" and the "Silent White Devil." For thirteen danger-filled years, this slim, boyish-looking soldier was the chief guardian of the Texas frontier. Idolized by his men, Hays was a Texas Ranger captain at age twenty-three, a major at twenty-five, and a colonel at thirty-one. His exploits made him a legendary figure, but Jack remained shy, modest, and unassuming — a hero who blushed when complimented. After he gained national fame in the Mexican War, a Texas county was named in his honor in 1848. Economic opportunity soon lured Hays to California, where he became sheriff of San Francisco County, a founder and developer of the city of Oakland, and the surveyor general of the state. Although riches and social-political prominence came his way in California, Jack's dying words attest to his love for Texas.

His grandfather, Robert Hays, was of Scotch-Irish descent and grew up in Rockbridge County, Virginia. After serving as a lieutenant in the North Carolina infantry during the Revolutionary War, Robert moved to Wilson County, Tennessee, in 1785, and became one of the wealthiest residents in the Nashville area. A brother-in-law of Andrew Jackson, he sold the Hermitage to Old Hickory. One of his sons, Harmon Hays, served as an officer under General Jackson in the Creek War and the War of 1812. Fighting with the dragoons of Gen. John Coffee, Harmon faced the center of the British charge in the Battle of New Orleans. After marrying Elizabeth Cage, the couple named their second child for Harmon's former commanding officer. John Coffee Hays, or "Jack," as grandfather Robert first called him, was born on January 28, 1817, near Little Cedar Lick, Tennessee.

Jack's grand aunt was Rachel Donelson Jackson, and family social life centered about her home, the Hermitage. There the lad had many opportunities to hear tales spun by General Jackson. Growing up in the same section of Tennessee as the McCullochs and Sam Houston, young Hays mastered riding and shooting and developed exceptional running speed and endurance.

Tragedy struck the family in 1832 when Jack lost both his father and mother to yellow fever in a matter of weeks, leaving seven orphaned children. Along with his youngest sister and brother, Sarah and Robert, fifteen-year-old Jack was sent to live with their uncle, Robert Cage, on his plantation in Yazoo County, Mississippi. After hiring out as a chain boy and learning to survey, Hays performed this dangerous work for two years and saved enough money to attend Davidson Academy at Nashville for a year. When an illness during the long winter forced him to return to Mississippi, he tried to persuade his uncle to send him to West Point. Robert Cage determined that business would be a better career, however, so Jack "peacefully left home" at age nineteen. By this time, he stood five feet nine inches tall, weighed 150 pounds, and was described as having a Roman nose, piercing hazel eyes, and reddish brown hair.

Hearing of the fall of the Alamo and the Goliad Massacre in the spring of 1836, Jack decided to help the Texians in their revolution against Mexico. He used his surveying money to buy a fine horse, a good knife, and a brace of pistols. At New Orleans, he joined ninety volunteers from Kentucky, Mississippi, and Louisiana, who arrived at Nacogdoches soon after the Battle of San Jacinto. In a bar there a desperado decided to pick a fight with the quiet, slender newcomer. After knocking a drink from Jack's hand, the bully reached for his gun; in an instant Hays drew his pistol and killed the thug. He then rode to the home of an old family friend, Isaac Donahoe, who lived on Clear Creek near present Hempstead.

After being told where to find the Texas army, he proceeded to join these troops under the command of Gen. Thomas J. Rusk. Enlisting as a private, Jack was assigned to a spy company, with his first duty being to help bury the remains of Fannin's 350 men at Goliad. When all the volunteers were furloughed, Hays, with a letter of introduction from President Jackson in hand, paid a visit to President Sam Houston at Columbia. It was Houston who advised him to join the Ranger company that Capt. Erastus "Deaf" Smith was recruiting for service on the southwestern frontier, an area plagued by bandits and Comanches.

In early December 1836, Jack Hays became one of Smith's first recruits in a mounted company of 208 Rangers. Each enlisted for twelve months, furnished his own horse, rifle, and pistols, and was paid thirty dollars a month plus subsistence. While the unit trained and camped for four weeks on the San Antonio River, Captain Smith received his first orders; since the Mexican town of Laredo was the only settlement on the north bank of the Rio Grande, his company was to claim Texas jurisdiction there by raising a flag of independence on the town's church spire. In mid-February 1837, Deaf moved twenty Rangers to a new camp on the Medina River, where they lost a remuda of horses. Returning to San Antonio, they helped bury the ashes and charred fragments of the Alamo defenders with military honors on February 25.

When Smith departed for Laredo on March 6, Hays

was one of his twenty men. After traveling ten days, they reached the Chacon five miles east of town and learned of a large Mexican garrison in Laredo. On March 17, the Rangers were attacked by forty Mexican dragoons sent out from town, who surrounded and assaulted Deaf's defensive position in a mesquite thicket. In the forty-five-minute battle that followed, the Mexicans suffered ten killed and ten wounded before retreating, while only two Texians were wounded. Realizing the futility of contesting such a superior force in Laredo, Captain Smith ordered his men back to San Antonio, where they received a very cool reception.

The Laredo Expedition marked the first Ranger appearance west of the Nueces River and started a bitter ten-year struggle by Texas and Mexico to claim the disputed area. In recognition of his scouting efforts during this venture, Jack was promoted to sergeant.

Having served with Smith for four months, Hays transferred to the Ranger company of Capt. Henry Karnes. President Houston furloughed all but 600 of the Texas army in May 1837, leaving frontier defense in the hands of militia and Ranger companies. In 1838 Jack served as both a soldier and surveyor in the San Antonio area. He was appointed deputy surveyor of the Bexar District under R. C. Trimble and located seventy-six headright certificates that year. In August, Hays was one of twenty Rangers who joined Karnes on a scout to the Arroyo Seco, where they were attacked three times by 200 mounted Comanches. Although arrows killed all of their horses, Jack singled out the chief and killed him before the Indians retreated, leaving twenty dead warriors behind. It was after this battle that Hays adopted a Comanche maneuver. Like these Indians, he would charge, then recoil before a counter-offensive; the center of his line would fall back until the enemy was between two wings, at which time his flanking Rangers would meet pincerlike at the enemy's rear.

When not in the field on surveying expeditions, Jack

lived in San Antonio while making friends with both the Lipan and Delaware Indians. His most valuable ally was the young Lipan chief Flacco, who taught Hays to trail and copied every move of this Ranger who possessed some sort of charm and spell as a warrior. While surveying beyond Bexar, Jack struck up a friendship with some Delawares and agreed to join seventeen of them on a trapping excursion to the Pecos River. Traveling on foot and in pairs, they reached the Pecos, where one of their party was killed by a passing band of 100 Comanches. Thirsting for revenge, the Delawares voted to chase them down before the enemy could cross the Rio Grande into Mexico. Taking to the trail in a steady dog trot, the Delaware warriors and Hays ran for two days and nights, making only brief stops to eat, drink, or nap. At dawn on the third day, they attacked the surprised Comanche camp near the Rio Grande. Caught totally off-guard, the Comanches made a frantic dash for the river, but few managed to escape. During this total Delaware victory, Jack fought with only a knife and tomahawk.

On March 19, 1840, a delegation of sixty-five Comanches, including twelve chiefs, rode into San Antonio. Two months earlier, they had sent word that they wanted peace and were willing to return all their white captives, a number estimated to be 200. However, the Comanches brought with them only two prisoners, a small Mexican boy and a sixteen-year-old white girl named Matilda Lockhart, who was terribly bruised, burned, and scarred. The parley with the Texian commissioners took place at the Council House (courthouse) on the corner of Main Plaza and Market Street. Feeling deceived and angry because of Matilda's condition, the commissioners told the Comanche chiefs they would be held as hostages until *all* captives were brought in. Instantly, the Council House Fight erupted as the Indians shouted war whoops, drew their bows, rushed out into the square, and fled in all directions. In the chase that followed, thirty-three Comanches were killed, including all the chiefs, and the other thirty-two were captured and put in jail.

The bitter aftermath of this battle led to constant Comanche raids on San Antonio. Local citizens turned to Jack Hays, who organized the volunteer "Minute Men" to chase the marauders on short notice. One such member of his company was Samuel Maverick, a wealthy merchant and signer of the Texas Declaration of Independence. His wife Mary described the organization as follows:

> In the stable we built on our house lot, Mr. Maverick kept a fine blooded horse, fastened by a heavy padlocked chain to a mesquite-picket . . . This was the "war horse." . . . Each volunteer kept a good horse, saddle, bridle and arms, and a supply of coffee, salt, sugar and other provisions ready at any time to start on fifteen minutes warning, in pursuit of marauding Indians. At a certain signal given by the Cathedral bell, the men were off, in buckskin clothes and blankets responding promptly to the call.

In August 1840, Chief Buffalo Hump led between 500 and 1,000 Comanches and Kiowas in a raid to the Gulf Coast against Victoria and Linnville. After killing fifteen settlers in the Victoria area on August 6, the Indians attacked Linnville on Lavaca Bay two days later. Most of the residents scrambled into boats and escaped, but the warriors killed six others, burned the town, and looted the warehouse of John Joseph Linn. Dressed in his top silk hats, dress coats, boots, and carrying his umbrellas, the Indians retreated northward with 2,000 stolen horses and mules. As word of the coastal raid spread, some 200 Texian volunteers, including Hays and his Minute Men, gathered at Plum Creek, two miles south of present Lockhart, to intercept the Comanches as they retired to the plains. Led by Maj. Gen. Felix Huston, the Texians surrounded the Indians on August 12 and forced them into a fifteen-mile running fight, the Battle of Plum Creek, in which eighty-six Comanches and two Texians were killed. Although Hays did not distinguish himself in this victory, President Lamar rewarded him with a commission as Ranger captain at age twenty-three, with orders to enlist his own spy company to be stationed in San Antonio.

Evidently, Jack was quite comfortable in the dual role of soldier and surveyor. In February 1840, the citizens of San Antonio recommended him to President Lamar as being competent to survey the boundary of Travis County in which the new capital, Austin, was located. Local residents said this of Hays:

> He is a gentleman of purest character and of much energy and ability. He is by profession a surveyor, and has been employed as such in this county for the two last years and has shewn himself fully competent to any work in his line.

During that year he located eighty-nine land certificates, twenty-three of them on the Pedernales. In August 1841, he was elected county surveyor of Bexar County. Since Ranger scouting duties required so much of his time, deputies did much of the actual surveying.

The first company of Rangers that Captain Hays recruited at San Antonio in 1840 was soon considered the best outfit of Indian fighters on the frontier. His men had to own a horse worth at least one hundred dollars, have courage and good character, and be a good rider and shot. They wore *sombreros* as sun protectors, along with long leggings and long boots. The first Hays company included Henry E. McCulloch as lieutenant and Bigfoot Wallace as a private. Being in his unit was a dangerous life: half of them were killed every year.[1] Since Jack was

---

[1] One early recruit was "Alligator" Davis, who earned his nickname when the Ranger company camped on the Medina River. Angered because a surfaced, six-foot alligator seemed to be staring at him, the private remarked, "I'll take the critter out and muster him as a raw recruit." On his second effort, Davis locked his legs around the brute, held its jaws open with both hands, and brought it out on the bank.

empowered to declare martial law in the territory he patrolled, it became a customary Ranger practice to summarily execute captured felons, particularly horse thieves.

In the fall of 1840, some 200 Comanches were reported to be taking horses west of San Antonio. Their first test came when Hays's Ranger company caught up with the raiders at a crossing of the Guadalupe. Although outnumbered ten to one, Jack's men charged in spread-A formation, killed the chief, and forced his warriors to flee. After this daring attack, the Comanches were curious to know the name of such a formidable foe; soon they were calling him "Captain Yack." Later some Comanche chiefs were on the Main Plaza in San Antonio when Hays happened to ride by. Turning to his Lipan friend, Flacco, they asked why the Ranger captain would dare go alone into their hunting grounds, knowing there would be no help if he were attacked. Flacco responded by pointing to an Indian friend and saying, "Me and Blue Wing no afraid to go to hell togedder. Captain Yack, great brave, no afraid to go to hell by hisself."

In 1841 Hays led two daring reconnaissance patrols to the Laredo area. In February he took a small scouting party to check out rumors of Mexican troops being assembled there for an invasion of San Antonio. His Rangers saw few soldiers and were not challenged when they boldly rode through the streets of Laredo. To make a point about Mexican banditry and cattle stealing, Jack drove many Mexican horses back to his camp, only to return them the next morning along with a note that the Texians were willing to fight enemy troops but would not rob peaceful citizens. He explained that the horses had been seized "merely to let the Mexicans know that if we chose to retaliate the robbing which had been committed on the Americans, we were fully able to do it."

After the bandit Agatón Quinoñes attacked and robbed two traders near Laredo, Captain Hays set out in pursuit of the raiders on March 15, 1841. His party consisted of twelve Americans and thirteen Mexicans. Once spies carried the news to Laredo that the Texians were coming, Capt. Ignacio Garcia led his own twenty-five men and fifteen regular cavalry out to capture or drive off the *gringos*. On April 7, Hays's men were intercepted by the Mexicans about ten miles from Laredo. When a parley resulted in a Garcia ultimatum to surrender or be killed, Jack's men dismounted and charged 200 yards through thick underbrush before opening fire at close range. Seeing that their guns and marksmanship were inferior to that of the Texians, Garcia's men became demoralized and began to fall back. In the next hour, a series of mounted charges and retreats left nine Mexicans dead and twenty-five taken prisoner. Hays had only one man wounded and captured twenty-eight horses.

When Captain Garcia carried news of his defeat to Laredo, the *alcalde* came out with a white flag to beg the Texians to spare the town. Jack replied that the Rangers had only two demands: Turn over marauders Agaton and Manuel Leal, and give assurance that traders would be protected going to and from San Antonio. When the *alcalde* promised to meet these conditions, Hays released his prisoners.

San Antonio could now build and prosper under Ranger protection. When President Lamar visited the city in June 1841, some prominent citizens decided to stage a grand ball to honor Hays and his men after a long scout. Hostess Mrs. Yturri was pleased to hear that Jack and two young Ranger friends, Mike Chevaille and John Howard, would be able to attend. Attire was to be formal dress, which created a problem for the three honorees: they owned only one coat between them. After Maj. and Mrs. Juan Seguin opened the ball, some ladies noticed that Captain Hays entered first but was seen dancing only every third number. He would go to an adjoining room and take off the coat so his friends could take their turn dancing. Once their secret was known, the three

Rangers were told to relax, forget their dress, and enjoy *all* the dances.

That very month Jack took sixteen Rangers on a scout looking for Indian horse thieves. Seeing their signs near Uvalde Canyon, he left his men to reconnoiter and found twelve Indians camped, evidently scouts for the main body in advance. When they were discovered, the Indians broke for the protection of a dogwood thicket. The area was too dense for effective use of bow and arrow, but they did have one gun. After Hays and two other Rangers entered the thicket, one companion was killed and the other seriously wounded in the neck. Their leader carried the wounded man, Trueheart, to safety and then returned to the thicket alone. Fighting for almost three hours, Jack killed eleven Indians — including the last brave who had the gun — and took one squaw prisoner.

After returning to San Antonio for reinforcements, Hays's men were joined by Chief Flacco and his Lipan warriors in pursuing the main body of Indians. In the Battle of the Llano, Jack's force of twenty-five attacked the camp of some 100 braves. During the running fight, his spirited horse got out of control and carried him entirely through the Indian lines. Thinking that his friend was charging, Flacco followed. Both came out on the other side before riding around the flank to rejoin their comrades. Once the battle was over, Flacco remarked that he would not be left behind by anyone, but that Captain Yack was "*bravo* too much."

Only once did Hays lead his Rangers into an ambush, the Battle of Bandera Pass, but that fight also revealed his coolness under fire and ability to rally his men. After camping at the present site of Bandera in October 1841, his company marched ten miles toward Bandera Pass the next day. A large Comanche war party heading for the Medina Valley arrived there first, however, and laid an ambush for the Rangers in the narrow, long pass. Hiding behind brush and boulders on the steep slopes, the Comanches opened fire and charged once Jack's men were inside the south end of the pass. It seems that the surprised Rangers panicked and were about to lose control until their leader shouted, "Steady there, boys. Dismount and tie those horses; we can whip them — no doubt about that." During the next hour they returned a deadly fire and fought hand-to-hand before the Indians retreated to their tied horses at the north end of the pass. What had begun as a desperate situation ended with only five Rangers dead and five others wounded.

In the fall of 1841, Captain Hays was involved in a legendary one-hour standoff with 100 Comanches at Enchanted Rock. He first saw this 640-acre, pink granite mountain while surveying with twenty men at Crabapple Creek. The rock has a three-mile-round base, one sloping side, and a broad, flat top with a few shallow depressions.[2] By this time Jack had a small number of a new scarce and expensive weapon, the Colt five-shooter, .34-caliber, cap and ball revolver. Shortly after Samuel Colt received his first American patent in February 1836, he started production at Paterson, New Jersey,

---

[2] Two natural phenomena caused the Indians to be in awe of Enchanted Rock. They could hear strange, creaking noises on cool nights following hot days, sounds that geologists later attributed to the contraction of the rock's outer surface as it cooled from the heat of the day. The rock also appeared to glitter on clear, moonlit nights following a rain, due either to the moon shining on water trapped in the rock's indented surface, or to moonlight reflected from the wetted faces of feldspar minerals.

This natural wonder is eighteen miles north of Fredericksburg on Ranch Road 965, straddling the Gillespie-Llano county line. It was first discovered by Anglo Texans in 1829, when Capt. Henry S. Brown led a punitive expedition against raiding Indians. Enchanted Rock is the second largest outcropping of granite in the United States, surpassed only by Stone Mountain, Georgia. In 1971 it was designated a National Natural Landmark by the U.S. Department of the Interior's National Park Service. After being purchased by the Texas Parks and Wildlife Department in 1978, it was reopened to the public as Enchanted Rock State Natural Area in March 1984. Today a bronze plaque near the mountain crest commemorates Jack Hays's battle with the Comanches in 1841.

with the first model called the "Texas." Hays obtained his first Colt revolvers in 1839, either from merchant S. M. Swenson or trader David K. Torrey, both of whom had recently visited New York. The night before his ordeal on Enchanted Rock, Lt. Henry McCulloch watched Jack clean his revolvers and heard him prophetically say, "I may not need you; but if I do, I will need you mighty bad."

The next morning the Ranger captain scaled the rock alone to get a better view of the countryside. Taking his rifle, knife, and two Colts, he climbed the sloping side to the small summit. On the way down, Hays was jumped by ten Comanches; cut off, he dropped his compass, Jacob's rod, and chain, and scrambled back up the rock mountain. Hiding between two ledges, he slid into the shallow pit of a crater. He had lost his powder horn and thus had only eleven shots, but did have the advantage of a clear fire field down the slope. Since the rock was not good medicine to the Comanches, he felt sure he could hold out and kill the few who dared climb it until help arrived.

For the next hour there was a tense standoff as the Indians carefully peered above the rim of the crater and called his name. After killing one warrior with his rifle, Jack opened fire with the five-shooters and drove them back several times. Suddenly, there was a mass attack by 100 Comanches on the naked summit. Hays killed the first three who slid down into the crater. At that desperate moment the surveyors, who had heard the shots, came to his rescue and drove off the attackers. When it was all over, there were six dead Indians on the ground around Jack's position, with more at the base of the rock.

On December 8, 1841, the editor of the *Telegraph and Texas Register* noted that Captain Hays's efficient Ranger company had "almost completely broken up the old haunts of the Comanches in the vicinity of Bexar." The paper went on to declare,

So great has been the protection and security resulting

41

from the active enterprise of this excellent officer that the settlements are extending on every side around [San Antonio] and the country is assuming the appearance of peace and prosperity that characterized it previous to the revolution . . .

Partly in retaliation for President Lamar's Santa Fe Expedition of 1841, and to boost his waning popularity and prestige, Santa Anna twice sent Mexican troops into Texas in 1842. Early in the morning on March 5, Gen. Rafael Vasquez and 700 troops, including 400 regular cavalrymen, camped two miles from San Antonio and offered surrender terms. Saying that the city was impossible to defend, Mayor Juan Seguin chose to retire to his ranch. All of the Anglo families had fled town by March 1, leaving only 107 defenders in San Antonio. Most of these volunteers were from Gonzales, and they unanimously chose Hays to lead them. When a truce was declared until 2:00 P.M. on March 5, Jack held a council of war, and a vote was taken as to whether to fight or retreat. After a majority of the defenders voted to abandon the city, he led them to safety on the west bank of the Guadalupe opposite Seguin.

General Vasquez raised the Mexican flag over San Antonio but stayed only two days, long enough for his men to loot abandoned Anglo stores, warehouses, and homes. When his army began their retreat toward the Rio Grande on March 7, they carried off a dozen carts and 132 muleloads of plunder. Although Hays and his Rangers trailed the invaders beyond the Nueces, they lacked the strength to attack and returned to San Antonio. For reasons of economy, all Texas military forces were then disbanded except for Jack's spy company. He was ordered to increase his force to 150 men and to patrol the area between the San Antonio River and the Rio Grande, even though the state had no funds to pay them.

On September 10, 1842, Captain Hays learned that Brig. Gen. Adrian Woll and 1,300 regular Mexican troops were approaching San Antonio. While Jack was out scouting for him, Woll's army left the main road and entered the city through the hills. The Ranger leader returned at daylight on the eleventh, only to find the town surrounded and himself unable to re-enter. Although the Mexicans suffered twenty-four casualties in the fighting, Woll occupied the city that day and took fifty-three citizens prisoner, including the entire district court in session there. That night, Hays withdrew to the Guadalupe and sent out a call for troops to assemble at Seguin. The mayor of San Antonio, John W. Smith, also escaped and sent a note to Gonzales asking for help. Late on Monday, September 12, Matthew "Old Paint" Caldwell and eighty-five men arrived at Seguin. Caldwell, one of the recently released Santa Fe prisoners, was elected to command the volunteer force. Captain Hays was chosen to lead a scouting company of forty-two of the best mounted men, with Henry McCulloch as lieutenant.

By midnight on September 17, Caldwell's 210 men were camped on the east bank of Salado Creek, some six miles northeast of San Antonio and on the site of present Fort Sam Houston. Protected by a natural embankment and the dense timber of the Salado bottom, Caldwell's men could shoot into an open prairie to the east and northeast. "Old Paint" decided to make his stand in this location and to send Jack's company into town to draw out the enemy. Shortly after 9:00 on Sunday morning, September 18, Hays, McCulloch, and six other Rangers approached the Alamo at a gallop from the east; shouting insults and cutting capers, they challenged the enemy to come out and fight. When Captain Perez and 150 Mexican cavalrymen poured out of the mission compound in hot pursuit, Jack's men retreated toward Caldwell's position, crossing the Salado a mile above his camp. The Mexicans gathered on a hill 400 yards to the east of the Texian position. After a brief rest, Hays led his company in a long range skirmish with the Mexican cavalry. The enemy suffered ten killed and twenty-three wounded in

43

two charges before a cease-fire was ordered, and the Rangers returned to Caldwell's camp.

About 1:00 that afternoon, General Woll arrived with 400 infantry reinforcements, 160 more dragoons, and two artillery pieces. Thinking that an immediate attack would result in an easy victory, Woll formed his men in two battle lines — infantry and cavalry — on the prairie. For the next few hours, Caldwell sent out only fifteen to twenty men at a time to skirmish with the enemy. It was growing late when Woll ordered his infantry to make a frontal assault on the Texian position in the creek bottom. As they charged across the open prairie, protected marksmen dropped Mexicans by the score, most being hit in the head or breast. One of Caldwell's men remarked that "it was such an easy-going affair" and "seemed like child's play." Toward sunset, Woll reassembled his battered troops and ordered a retreat to San Antonio. During the daylong Battle of Salado, Colonel Caldwell lost only one man: Stephen Jett was killed by Indians who tried to steal his horse. Sixty Mexican bodies were left on the battlefield, while forty-four dead and 150 wounded troops were carried off. The next morning General Woll ordered a mass funeral in San Antonio rather than the planned grand victory *fandango*.

The Mexican invasion army evacuated the city on September 20. Two hundred Mexican families also fled under Woll's protection, taking 500 head of cattle and whatever plunder their carts would hold. At 10:00 that morning, Caldwell called a council of war, and a vote was taken to pursue the enemy and attack if possible, with Hays's Ranger company leading the way. While Woll's force camped six miles above present Castroville, Jack and Ben McCulloch decided to enter the encampment to gather intelligence. After dismounting, the two wrapped Mexican blankets around their bodies, pulled their hats down low, and strolled through the camp. The Rangers were back at their point of entry when a sentry barked, "Who goes there?" Jack whipped out his pistol and retorted, "Texians, damn you!" While he was disarming the sentry to take him prisoner, Hays told Ben, "He won't shoot. I judge by his voice that he is scared." The two then took their prize back to Caldwell's camp on the Medina River. This audacious episode caused a Mexican general to put a price of $500 on Jack's head.

Captain Hays wanted to attack before the enemy reached the Hondo, but Colonel Caldwell's 500 citizen volunteers were fearful of the artillery protecting the Mexican rear. At 3:00 P.M. on September 22, Jack's company caught up with Woll's rearguard near the Arroyo Hondo. By then the Mexican army had crossed the river and assumed a defensive position on the west side. General Woll had just recrossed the Hondo with 100 infantrymen and fifty cavalry to protect the Mexican families and his two cannon on the east side. His eyes blazing, Hays was given permission to assault the cannon. Caldwell promised to support his charge.

As Jack and his fifty volunteers made a mad 400-yard dash toward their objective, cannon fire overshot them, and the Rangers killed all five Mexicans manning the artillery as they passed by. When Woll threw Mexican women and children into the space between the captured cannon and his main army, Hays's men had to fall back as the Mexican infantry advanced. At this critical point, Caldwell failed to support the attack "owing to the boggy situation of the ground and tired horses." All Jack had to show for his heroic effort was five wounded Rangers. It was said that he cried tears of shame and rage the next morning when Maj. James Mayfield, who had belatedly joined the Texians with 100 volunteers from Bastrop and Travis counties, made a speech which led to an order to discontinue the pursuit. Woll's worn-out, dispirited army slipped away during the night and reached the Rio Grande on October 1.

After first refusing to obey the order to return to San Antonio, Hays's company was the last to come in. Awaiting him was a letter from President Houston, dated September 14, promoting Jack to major. Further dispatches authorized him to take command and to declare martial law in Bexar County.

When Caldwell's forces reached San Antonio on September 24, they gathered in front of the Alamo to hear a speech by Vice-President Edward Burleson, who urged them to go home, get fresh provisions and horses, then return to San Antonio a month later. On October 3, 1842, President Houston ordered Brig. Gen. Alexander Somervell of Matagorda to take command of Texas troops gathering at San Antonio. He was to patrol the Rio Grande and was given broad discretionary powers to invade Mexico if he thought it could be successfully done. Seeking to take advantage of Jack's scouting talents, Houston told Somervell, "You may rely upon the gallant Hays and his companions; and I desire that you should obtain his services and cooperation."

On November 7, the volunteers concentrated at Mission San Jose to organize into companies and regiments. Jack's regular Ranger company consisted of sixty men, with Henry McCulloch serving as first lieutenant. Joining these scouts was a small group of Lipans led by Chief Flacco, who received the title of colonel and a full-dress uniform. On November 25, Somervell's force of 750 men, many of them self-willed and undisciplined adventurers, moved out from their camp near the Medina. The troops had no wagons and were short on powder, lead, beef, and bread. Leading the way was Hays's spy company, which carried a flag made by Mrs. Eleanor Elliot of San Antonio, with the motto, "We give but ask no quarter." By this time General Somervell had called a council of war and decided to march against Laredo, which was not as heavily guarded as San Fernando de Rosas, where Gen. Isidro Reyes had 800 troops.

After three days in the bogs, the Texian army reached the Laredo road and crossed the Frio on December 1. Upon reaching the flooded Nueces, Jack's scouts undressed and swam their horses across the river with revolvers and belts around their necks and rifles held high. Hays then persuaded Somervell to build a crude bridge across the main channel so the main army could cross on foot. After finding no Mexican forces at Laredo, Jack suggested that the town be taken by a forced march. By daybreak on December 8, the Texians were in a semicircle around the city. Only hours earlier, the Mexican garrison had crossed to the west bank of the Rio Grande, and the *alcalde* had driven off 1,000 horses and mules. When Somervell and Hays led the parade into Laredo that morning, they received a friendly greeting from the residents, and Jack hoisted the Texas flag on the church steeple.

That afternoon the Texians relocated three miles below Laredo at Camp Chacon, a high hill near the river. On the morning of December 9, about one-third of the troops reentered Laredo and plundered the town, taking what they pleased from Mexican families. Although Somervell returned the booty — a pile the size of "a good large house" — to the *alcalde* and apologized for the misconduct of "some bad men belonging to the army," he kept all the pilfered coffee, flour, saddles, soap, and sugar.

After the troops marched through ten miles of dense chaparral down the east bank of the Rio Grande, General Somervell addressed his men on December 11, and 187 chose to return home after being given permission to do so. The rest of the army — some 500 men — elected Somervell as "volunteer leader" and moved across the Rio Grande to near Guerrero, some sixty miles below Laredo. On December 15, Somervell demanded that the *alcalde* of Guerrero provide 100 horses and five days' provisions for 1,200 men. When no horses and only ten pounds each of sugar and coffee were provided the next morning, the Texian leader ordered a retreat to the opposite bank of the river and camped near the town of Zapata.

On the morning of December 17, Somervell ordered Hays to demand $5,000 of the *alcalde,* or else Guerrero would be sacked. Only fifty-two men from the spy companies of Jack and Capt. Samuel Bogart volunteered for this dangerous mission. For ninety tense minutes, Hays's men formed three sides and fronted the center of the main square. Then the *alcalde* appeared with only $381 of silver tied in a handkerchief. The angry Ranger leader refused to accept that paltry sum, arrested the *alcalde,* and took him to Somervell after withdrawing his men. With all of his men now on the east side of the Rio Grande, Somervell decided that sacking Guerrero was not worth the effort. On the morning of December 19, he backed down, abandoned the whole operation, and ordered the army to march for the settled areas of Texas and disband at Gonzales.

Cursing their leader, many of the men "became perfectly wild," and five captains refused to obey the order. When one of them, William S. Fisher, asked permission to separate from the expedition and march down the river, Somervell refused the request. This stalemate prompted 305 officers and men to withdraw from the command and choose Fisher to lead them in a private war, an expedition into the interior against Mier, Mexico.

Most of Hays's Ranger outfit were among the 189 men who started for Gonzales at 1:00 P.M. on December 19, but Samuel Walker and Bigfoot Wallace chose to stay with Fisher. Jack stayed a few days to perform scouting duties for the Mier Expedition but left for San Antonio before dawn on December 24. After traveling a hundred miles, he discovered that his fine gift horse from Tennessee had bolted free and headed for the Rio Grande. After trailing him to a Mexican ranch on the river, Hays slipped into the stable after dark and retrieved his mount. En route home he discovered the body of his friend Flacco, who had been killed by Mexican horse thiefs. By early January 1843, Jack was back in San Antonio to resume his independent command there.

An act of the Texas Congress on January 16 authorized Hays to raise a new company of twenty Rangers. In April, President Houston placed the territory between the Frio and Nueces rivers and the Rio Grande under military law. Jack spent much of this time scouting for the notorious Mexican bandit Agaton, who was in terror of the Ranger major. After learning that some traders had killed Agaton in early November, Hays furloughed his Ranger company. While visiting in Seguin at Thanksgiving, he began to court Susan Calvert, the slender, dark-haired daughter of Judge Jeremiah H. Calvert, from Florence, Alabama.

While visiting with President Houston in early January 1844, Jack was told that the Texas navy had received a supply of the new Colt five-shooter. He was allowed to place an order with the secretary of war to equip his new Ranger company of forty privates that was to operate from Bexar to Refugio counties and west. After obtaining the prized weapons at Galveston, Hays returned to San Antonio, called together his disbanded company, and issued each of them two of the revolvers.

Early that spring he took fifteen Rangers on a three-week scout to the north. While returning to San Antonio, they decided to rob a bee tree at Sister Creek near the Guadalupe. When he was thirty feet above the ground, John Coleman noticed twenty-five Comanches sitting on their horses some 300 yards away. Jack ordered a Ranger charge, only to stop within sixty yards of the Indians when he saw two other lines of warriors on a hill behind them. As Hays's men dashed for some timber and dismounted, they were chased by the first row as the last two lines fanned to both sides. After circling the grove time after time, the three Comanche parties finally charged. Eight Rangers were seriously wounded in the battle, but the Indians retreated, carrying their dead and wounded, after Ad Gillespie killed their war chief.

In March 1844, Chief Buffalo Hump and fifty Comanche warriors rode into San Antonio seeking a peace treaty. Major Hays suggested a rodeo with his Rangers, the Comanches, and Mexican *rancheros* as participants. Choosing a prairie near the Main Plaza as the rodeo arena, he served as master of ceremonies and awarded pistols and Bowie knives as prizes. Although the judges gave each Indian contestant a present in the "riding match," the first prize for horsemanship went to a Ranger, John McMullin, with Comanche brave Long Quiet winning second place. Jack did not take part in the contest, but a contemporary said this of him:

> As a horseman . . . he was . . . able to ride at full speed and pick up a half dollar from the ground with his hand. No Comanche could surpass him in throwing his body from one side of his horse to the other, and thus dodging Indian arrows and sometimes bullets.

When the rodeo was over, Buffalo Hump told Hays to get married and have many papooses to carry on "Devil Yack's" name; he even suggested that the first-born be called Buffalo Hump, Jr.

The Battle of Walker's Creek in present Kendall County was to prove the effectiveness of the Rangers' new Colt revolvers. On June 8, 1844, Hays and fourteen men camped on Walker's Creek, equidistant from Austin, Gonzales, and San Antonio. There they encountered Chief Yellow Wolf and seventy-five Comanche warriors, who withdrew to the top of a brush-covered, steep peak, dismounted in a battle line, and shouted insults in Spanish at the Rangers. Unintimidated, Jack shouted back to the chief, "Yellow Dog, son of a dog-mother, the Comanche's liver is white!" Rather than being goaded into scaling the hill, however, Hays led his undetected man along the dry-bottomed ravine and skirted the hill to attack from the rear. Forming a V-shaped wedge, they charged the surprised Indians from the prairie side of the peak. During a two-mile Comanche retreat, Yellow Wolf rallied his braves for three attacks with the Rangers fighting in relays. Just as the chief prepared for a final rally, Ad Gillespie shot him through the head at thirty yards, and his demoralized warriors fled. In all, the running fight covered three miles and lasted an hour. One Ranger was killed and four were wounded, while the Indians suffered twenty-three dead along with thirty seriously wounded. On June 23, the Houston *Morning Star* ran an account of the fight which praised the skill, courage, and modesty of Hays.

The new Colt revolvers were so deadly in the Battle of Walker's Creek that the Rangers fired only 150 shots; in fact, Jack attributed the victory to the five-shot pistol. (Later-model Colts bore an engraving of the battle scene stamped on the cylinders. Based on a sketch by participant Samuel Walker, the action scene shows Rangers chasing Comanches, with Hays on a white horse and Walker on a black one.)

The summer of 1844 found Jack and his men escorting and protecting the advance guard of the French-Swiss colonists sent by Henri Castro to found a settlement west of the Medina River. The generous Ranger leader even used his own credit so that those stranded on the Texas coast could have wagon transportation to San Antonio. His services prompted the grateful Castro to observe, "Major Hays and his noble companions . . . were equal to any emergency, but such a company can, in my opinion, only be compared to the old musketeers . . . of France." When Prince Carl of Solms-Braunfels was sent by the German Adelsverein (Society of Nobles) to found a colony in Texas, he was escorted to the headquarters site, New Braunfels, by Major Hays. The prince also praised him as "perhaps the only one from whom accurate information of the mountainous regions can be obtained."

Dividing his men into small platoons enabled Jack to protect these new frontier settlements. Only a man with his iron constitution could ride out with one platoon, return to camp, then lead another scout with the rested group. Despite their yeoman service, Hays had to furlough his company due to lack of appropriations. When the new settlements complained to new President Anson Jones, he persuaded the Texas Congress to expand Hays's Rangers, and new recruits were mustered in for six months' service in early February 1845.

After the Texas Congress approved terms of annexation offered by the United States in June 1845, President James K. Polk sent Gen. Zachary Taylor and his Federal troops from Fort Jesup, Louisiana, to the mouth of the Nueces in July. At the time, Taylor recommended that the Rangers continue to defend the Texas frontier. When an act of the U.S. Congress recognized the Rio Grande as the southwestern boundary of Texas in late December 1845, Major Hays traveled from his San Antonio headquarters to visit General Taylor at Corpus Christi. Jack had heard that Taylor was about to move his troops to the Rio Grande and offered to put his Rangers under the general's orders for scouting purposes. Initially, Taylor declined, but experience soon proved that his own dragoons could not handle the task. By the time he reached Fort Brown on the Rio Grande, and even before the U.S. Congress declared war on Mexico, Taylor was asking for 5,000 Texas volunteers — two regiments of infantry and two of cavalry.

It was during this interlude that Hays had his last major encounter with Texas Indians, the Battle of Painted Rock, in present Llano County. While he was in Corpus Christi, some 600 Comanches raided southwest of San Antonio, and a Ranger detail caught up with the retreating marauders at Enchanted Rock. A fresh trail indicated that the Comanches were heading for a major watering hole, a small lake at the base of Painted Rock. Facing odds of fifteen to one, Jack took forty Rangers, rode 130 miles in forty-two hours, and reached the lake ahead of the Indians at 1:00 in the morning. His men hid in a thicket of willow trees on the north shore of the small lake, the *only* approach to that watering hole. On the south rim was Painted Rock, rising some hundred feet above the lake.

Bone-tired after their long ride, the Comanches approached at early dawn, expecting to make camp there. Although they retreated as the Rangers opened fire, the trail they spotted showed that there were only a few white foes;

the confident Indians could afford to wait until daybreak, then overwhelm the Rangers by sheer numbers.

Their first line of attack formed to the northeast of the willow thicket. The sight of 600 charging Comanches — with their short bows, inpenetrable shields, and fourteen-foot lances — filled a sixteen-year-old Ranger, F. W. Harrison, with terror. When they were within fifty yards, Hays ordered his men to open fire, and the braves galloped by the thicket while unloosing a barrage of arrows. Hiding behind their racing horses, the warriors swung into a half circle and made a second charge past the grove of trees. After trying a third tactic, a lance charge, the Comanches made intermittent attacks throughout the day before withdrawing to camp on the prairie that night. Desperate for water, they were forced to send a party twenty miles to get it. The next morning the Indians attacked in four successive waves, with some from the final group managing to crash in the grove's edge. Then they tried firing their arrows from the top of Painted Rock; they were ineffective from that range, but Ranger bullets did find their mark. At dusk the warriors withdrew again and sent for water.

On the third morning all attacks came from the north at different angles, forcing Jack's men to divide their fire. Realizing that the Rangers' ammunition supply was running low, the Comanche war chief decided to lead his braves in a final, suicidal assault at 10:00. Just as the charge began, the chief made a fatal mistake; as he swung around to shout orders, his rawhide shield turned with him, exposing his side. At that instant Hays killed him with a single rifle shot. As the Indians retreated, Jack ordered one of his men to rope the chief's neck and drag the corpse back to Ranger lines. The furious Comanches then charged one final time before fleeing to the northwest, leaving over 100 of their dead on the battlefield. Incredibly, only one Ranger, Emory Gibbons, was wounded and one horse was killed by a shower of arrows.

When Jack and his men returned to camp near San

Antonio on March 18, 1846, he learned that General Taylor's men were advancing to a new position on the Rio Grande opposite Matamoros, Mexico. Once hostilities commenced with 1,600 Mexican troops on the north bank of the river on April 25, Taylor asked Texas Governor J. Pinckney Henderson for four volunteer regiments the next day. Since his supply base was twenty-five miles away at Point Isabel, Taylor also mustered two of Hays's Ranger companies — led by Samuel Walker and Ben McCulloch — into national service to keep his communications open.

While Governor Henderson recruited his infantry regiment, Jack was given a much-needed leave that spring and spent the time renewing his courtship of Susan Calvert, who was visiting her cousin, Mrs. Elizabeth Riddle, in San Antonio. Susan had promised to be his bride by the time Mrs. Riddle hosted a farewell ball for Hays's light cavalry regiment.

The two volunteer mounted regiments were commanded by Jack and Col. George T. Wood, whose men came from the interior and East Texas. Hays had the hardened frontiersmen, experienced Mexican and Indian fighters who were killers intent on using the war to avenge past treatment at the hands of the Mexicans. Terrified Mexican civilians had good reason to fear these men; deep hatred had festered for ten years, and some Rangers would spend much of their time rooting out and dispatching old enemies. One of them sarcastically wrote of having strict orders not to molest any unarmed Mexican; according to this Texian, any notorious villain found shot or hung must have committed suicide during a fit of remorse, tortured by conscience for his evil deeds.

Jack Hays was elected colonel of a unit officially called the First Regiment Texas Mounted Rifles, but popularly known as Hays's Texas Rangers. Samuel H. Walker was chosen as lieutenant colonel and Michael Chevaille was elected major when the eight companies assembled at Point Isabel on June 22, 1846. They drew equipment there, including army-size Colt revolvers with extra cylinders, but refused to wear army uniforms. Their "uniform" was an odd, colorful assortment of clothes, usually a dirty red or blue shirt, and a wide variety of hats.

Except for the clean-shaven Colonel Hays, the Rangers wore long beards and mustaches, and made it a point to look — and act — as ferocious as possible. Each was armed with a short rifle or shotgun, holster pistols, Colt five-shooters, and a Bowie knife. They rode on horses, asses, mustangs, and mules. Samuel Chamberlain, an artist-soldier in the Mexican War, said that "with their uncouth costumes, bearded faces, lean and brawny forms, fierce wild eyes and swaggering manners, they were fit representatives of the outlaws which make up the population of the Lone Star State." After camping at Matamoros on August 2, the fully armed Rangers received curious stares from other volunteers when they barged into a local theater.

Because of his confidence in the scouting ability of the Rangers, General Taylor assigned Ben McCulloch's company to determine the best U.S. invasion route to Monterrey. Finding that the direct, planned route by way of Linares — the one taken by General Arista and the retreating Mexican army — lacked the water holes to support an army, McCulloch suggested that the Americans go by way of the Rio Grande and the San Juan River. Following his advice, Taylor in mid-August took only 6,640 men, half of them his trusted regulars, and moved toward Monterrey by way of Mier, Camargo, and Cerralvo at the edge of the Sierra Madre. At the same time, he ordered Colonel Hays and the major part of his regiment to parallel his column, scout the Linares route for 130 miles as far as San Fernando, then join the main army.

Jack's Rangers left Matamoros on August 5 and reached China twenty days later, effectively "buying" mules for Taylor's men as he went. Quartermaster Henry Whiting, who had demanded twenty mules from each town *alcalde,* later admitted, "This call might have been ineffectual, had not a Texian mounted regiment [Colonel Hays's] been moving into the quarter whence we expected these mules. A regiment will make that possible which might otherwise be deemed impossible." While camped at China, Jack shot a horse thief as an example.

During this time Taylor's main army was concentrating at Cerralvo across the San Juan Valley. On September 13, the two converging columns began their move on Monterrey, with Hays's men moving from China by way of Caderita. Five days later he joined the main body of the army at San Francisco. On Saturday, September 19, General Taylor's army reached a slope overlooking Monterrey, three miles to the southwest, and made camp at Walnut Springs, a delightful grove of pecans and live oaks that served as the picnic grounds of the city. Facing him was an impregnable stronghold where Cuban General Pedro de Ampudia had massed 7,300 troops. Confronting Taylor northeast of the city was the Citadel, a walled fortress with eight cannon and surrounded by a moat. On the south, Monterrey was protected by the Santa Catarina River and mountains. To the west, and guarding the road to Saltillo, were two steep, fortified hills, Independencia and Federacion. Within the fortified interior of the city, the Mexicans had placed sandbag parapets on the flat roofs and cut loopholes in the stone walls for sharpshooters.

Taylor was incensed when some of the Rangers swarmed out of camp to display their horsemanship and courage by riding back and forth in front of the Citadel's walls. It was his plan to form a battle line of the regulars and Colonel Wood's East Texas volunteer regiment in assaulting the northeast edge of the city, then fight house to house to the main plaza. At the same time, Gen. William Worth and two brigades of the 2nd Division, along with Hays's Ranger regiment, would march around the city to cut off any reinforcements from Saltillo. This risky strategy involved dividing the American strength between opposite ends of Monterrey.

Shortly after noon on Sunday, September 20, General Worth's column, headed by Jack's Texians, moved out. They had been instructed to make a wide sweep to the west, block the Saltillo road, cut off supplies, and take the two hills guarding the entrance to the city. As events were to prove, Worth's 2,000 men did all this and more. By 6:00 they were seven miles from Taylor and close to both the Saltillo road and the hidden guns on Independence Hill. While camping that rainy night, Worth sent a dispatch asking Taylor to support his dawn attack with a strong diversion at the opposite end of the city. Hays's men had to endure a pouring rain with no coats, blankets, or food; when questioned about their rations, Taylor is said to have remarked, "They'll find something over there."

At 6:00 the next morning, Worth's column followed the lead of the Rangers, who turned the angle of a hill to suddenly face a lancer regiment led by Lt. Col. Juan Najera. Brandishing his saber, Colonel Hays called out in Spanish and challenged Najera to a duel. Jack's action shocked his men, since the Ranger was deadly with a pistol but unskilled with the saber. The Mexican leader eagerly accepted the challenge, drew his long saber, and charged. As they raced toward each other, Hays abruptly swayed to the right, drew his Colt revolver, fired under his horse's neck, and killed Najera with a single shot. He then galloped back to his men and shouted, "Dismount! Get behind your horses! Here they come, boys. Give 'em hell!" As Sgt. Buck Barry remembered it, the Mexicans charged "like mad hornets," passing through the Ranger lines three times. Protected by their horses, the Rangers shot down eighty of them at close range and lost only one man.

After learning that the enemy was advancing to protect the Saltillo road, Hays dismounted five of his companies and set up an ambush along the road. Capt. Ben McCulloch's company then feigned a retreat, chased by

1,500 Mexican cavalrymen who raced right into the ambush with the dismounted Rangers pouring fire into them from a distance of ten to twenty yards. When Ben's men counterattacked, the enemy retreated after suffering 100 killed or wounded. Jack had only eight casualties in what General Worth described as a "beautiful maneuver." The Americans had secured the Saltillo road, but Worth was eight miles from the main army with no communications, only four days' rations, and a superior force before him.

Monterrey was now in view, with the two fortified hills on either side in the foreground. Worth decided to first take the one south of the Saltillo road, Federation Hill, after Hays convinced him that it could be stormed. Early that afternoon, six companies of Rangers and an equal number from the Fifth and Seventh infantry regiments started up the hill in three waves at intervals. By midafternoon the combined force had overrun Fort Soldado, a large gun emplacement at the western end of Federation Hill, with Capt. Ad Gillespie's Ranger company being the first to mount the enemy's works. Colonel Hays reported that only two Rangers were killed and nine wounded in taking the 400-foot-high peak.

The next day, September 22, General Worth's men achieved one of the greatest victories of the Mexican War by taking the opposite parallel peak, Independence Hill, and the Bishop's Palace, bristling with cannon and the key to Monterrey's western defense. At 3:00 A.M. an attacking force of 500, including seven Ranger companies, started up the 800-foot, almost vertical peak. Since the upper, western end was fortified, General Ampudia had assumed it to be unassailable and thus posted no guards there. Hays and Samuel Walker led two columns up the northwest and southwest slopes, with Jack's men on the right and Sam's on the left. When dawn came, both Ranger leaders were within 100 yards of the battery on the summit when they were discovered and fired on. Twenty yards from the crest, they fanned out and returned fire as Jack shouted, "Give them hell!" After a short, desperate struggle, the Mexicans abandoned the battery and fled down the slope toward the Bishop's Palace. Captain Gillespie had just died while standing on the sandbags of the redoubt, so his Ranger companions stood in subdued silence as the American regulars raised the U.S. flag.

After dragging a twelve-pound howitzer up the steep slopes, Worth's men reassembled it at the top of Independence Hill. By noon they were throwing shells against the Bishop's Palace, and Worth had gathered 1,000 men for an attack. Fearing Mexican reinforcements from the city and a possible counteroffensive, Colonel Hays suggested an old Comanche trap to lure the enemy out of the palace. The Rangers formed in two concealed, forward positions along each side of the ridge, with Jack's men on the right, Walker's on the left, and the regulars behind them. When a Mexican infantry and cavalry sortie formed in front of the palace, all they could see before them was an advance by Captain Blanchard's Louisiana company which opened fire, then retreated with the enemy lancers and infantry eagerly giving chase. Suddenly, the two flanking Ranger columns blasted the Mexicans from each side of the ridge before closing the gap behind the enemy. Amid mass confusion, the Mexicans broke formation and fled downhill toward the city, leaving their artillery behind. By 4:00 that afternoon, the few defenders left in the Bishop's Palace had surrendered. With a remarkable victory achieved, Hays took his Rangers back to the junction of the Saltillo and Topo roads, where he reported only two dead and six wounded.

Although General Taylor had begun operations on the northeastern end of the city, it was the loss of the Bishop's Palace that caused General Ampudia to begin a withdrawal into the center of Monterrey, thus leaving the outer city blocks undefended by dawn of September 23. That afternoon, 400 dismounted Rangers joined General Worth's 7th and 8th Infantry in street and house-to-house fighting. Attacking from the west along two parallel streets, Hays led the right-hand column down the Calle de Monterrey while Walker and the left wing of Rangers swept down Iturbide Street. At the Cemetery Plaza they encountered their first resistance from sharpshooters on housetops, prompting Jack to divide his men into six groups, and pick them off with an accurate pattern of crossfire.

Since Mexican bullets and grapeshot were sweeping the through streets, the two Worth columns had the wit to advance *through* buildings. A Ranger would pick a hole in the soft stone of a house's side, insert a shell with a three-second fuse, and blow out a wide opening; troops then rushed in, cleared out snipers, and the process was repeated at the next house. At 4:00 General Taylor withdrew his eastern force across town, enabling the Mexican defenders to concentrate on Worth's men. Even though they were fighting alone, the two Ranger-led columns were within a block of the grand plaza by sundown on Wednesday.

The next morning, Walker's men resumed firing from rooftops while Hays's column reoccupied the southwestern section of the city. By 10:00 the Rangers had trapped the enemy with the grand plaza, the streets leading to it, the cathedral, and the main highway under their rifles. They were within hours of forcing unconditional surrender when General Ampudia hoisted a white flag and sought a brief armistice to work out surrender details. After suspending the advance, General Taylor ordered a cease-fire which extended to a truce during the day. The Texians were angry and disappointed by Taylor's liberal terms, whereby Ampudia surrendered Monterrey but was allowed to withdraw his armed, intact Mexican garrison to the mountains to enjoy an eight-week truce. Such terms brought a storm of criticism down on Taylor and violated his orders from an angry President Polk.

With their task completed, Colonel Hays ordered his men back to their camp at the road junction. During the

Monterrey campaign, only seventy of General Worth's men were killed or wounded, compared to 800 casualties for General Taylor. Although Worth was promoted to brevet major general for cracking the crucial western defense of Monterrey, he gave due credit to an important ally. On September 28, he expressed his admiration for "the distinguished gallantry of Colonel Hays and his noble band of volunteers. Hereafter they and we are brothers, and we can desire no better security of success than by their association." Worth also declared that Hays's Rangers were "the best light troops in the world" and said that "Jack Hays is the tallest man in the saddle in front of the enemy I ever saw."

Before the regiment was mustered out of service, Worth asked Jack's men to have wine at his headquarters. He shook hands with each man and told Hays, "It was the untiring, vigorous bravery, and unerring shots of your regiment that saved my division from defeat." For his part, the modest Ranger leader offered a succinct explanation for his Monterey success: "They [the Mexicans] were damn poor shots."

Once Monterrey was secured, Taylor decided to discharge the Texas volunteer regiments. He did not want to be responsible for their behavior during weeks of inactivity; also, some of the companies had three-month enlistments about to expire. By October 2, 1846, all companies of Hays's First Mounted Rifles had been mustered out. During the week before they rode for Texas, army officer Luther Giddings observed that some Rangers displayed a "lawless and vindictive spirit" and expressed the hope that "all honest Mexicans were at a safe distance from their path" as they headed home.

Although General King praised Jack's men as "not only the eyes and ears of General Taylor's army, but its right and left arms as well," Zachary detested their lack of discipline and violent ways, describing them as being a "lawless set" and "too licentious to do much good." He wrote that "the mounted men from Texas have scarcely made one expedition without unwarrantably killing a Mexican." On another occasion, he said of them, "On the day of battle, I am glad to have Texas soldiers with me, for they are brave and gallant; but I never want to see them before or afterward." On June 16, 1847, he went so far as to specifically request that the adjutant general send no more Rangers to his column.

Colonel Hays returned to a hero's welcome at San Antonio. The most popular man in Texas, he was also showered with praise by newspapers throughout the United States. On November 7, 1846, Acting Governor A. C. Horton authorized him to organize another regiment, and Jack asked Major Chevaille to raise it in his absence. Samuel Walker, his second-in-command at Monterrey, had been appointed a captain in the U.S. Army, First Regiment of Mounted Riflemen, and General Taylor ordered him to report to the adjutant general at Washington after the Texians were discharged. Since Jack had business in Mississippi, the two traveled together as far as New Orleans, where their arrival created a sensation. After arriving at the capital about November 20, Walker went on to New York, where he received a letter from the bankrupt Samuel Colt asking him to persuade the president and secretary of war to approve Colt's weapons for both Hays's new regiment and Walker's riflemen.[3]

---

[3] Ranger experience on the Texas frontier had revealed problems with the original model Paterson Colt revolver. The weapon had no trigger guard and a concealed trigger which dropped into view when the revolver was cocked. While being loaded, it had to be broken down to three pieces; the barrel had to be removed to replace an empty cylinder with a full one. Thus a Ranger on horseback could not reload the five-shooter.

When Walker met Colt in New York, he told the inventor of these defects, and that his weapon was far too light and flimsy for frontier use. After the two Sams talked far into the night, Colt had the ideas for a new pistol and an agreement was reached: Colt would modify his revolvers while Walker would press the government to buy them. On January 4, 1847, a contract was signed whereby the United States

Jack was back in San Antonio by December 1846, where he found only enough recruits to muster four companies. The problem was getting men to enlist for the duration of the war. On January 1, he conferred with Governor Henderson about the proposed regiment. The governor agreed to draft a letter to President Polk, suggesting the need for a specific term of service and expressing his concern about protecting the Texas frontier. On February 18, 1847, Henderson sent Hays to Washington as his personal representative to discuss both matters with the president and secretary of war. As a result of this mission, an order of March 20 authorized enlistments for one year in the proposed regiment, including those companies deemed necessary to protect the frontier.

While in Washington, Colonel Hays heard from Samuel Colt, who wanted him to see the improved six-shot revolver designed by Walker. Jack was assured that his regiment would get the major share of the first thousand new weapons once Walker's company was supplied. Before returning to Texas, Hays paid his respects to Mrs. Sarah Childress Polk, the wife of the president, who inquired about his Tennessee relatives and saw a picture of his Susan. On the evening of March 18, the famous Ranger attended the wedding of Senator Thomas Hart Benton's daughter, then escorted Mrs. Polk to the dining room after the ceremony.

Upon returning to San Antonio in early April 1847, Jack accepted command of a six-month volunteer regiment

---

government agreed to purchase 1,000 of the new pistols at $25 each. The pistols were to be delivered within six months. Eli Whitney, Jr., undertook the actual manufacture of the revolvers, and the first 220 were shipped to Captain Walker at Vera Cruz in July 1847.

This new model Colt revolver was referred to as the Walker Colt, the "Model of 1847 Army Pistol," or the "Old Army Type." The .47-caliber *six*-shooter had a stronger, heavier frame and thus served as an effective club. It had a visible trigger and guard, a longer cylinder, and a lever rammer below the barrel which seated bullets in the chamber without removing the cylinder — the best feature which allowed for reloading without dismounting.

being raised there. He and Susan were to be married at Seguin on April 29, and a carpenter had already started construction of their two-story home in the 200 block of South Presa Street. The couple were married in the bride's home by Reverend Doctor Anderson, a Presbyterian pastor, and the wedding reception was held in the Magnolia Hotel. Since Jack had only two weeks before leaving with his new regiment for Mexico, the newlyweds honeymooned at San Antonio, where his friends hosted a grand ball and supper in their honor. To keep him fighting trim, Hays would trot for miles alongside the buggy as he and Susan took long rides into the countryside.

After leaving San Antonio with his men on May 14, Colonel Hays received new orders from General Taylor upon reaching the Nueces. Learning that Taylor would accept enlistments only for the duration or twelve months, the chagrined Ranger leader took his regiment back to San Antonio and discharged them.

In the meantime, the focus of the Mexican War had shifted. In late November 1846, Secretary of War William Marcy ordered Senior General Winfield Scott to take command in Mexico and to initiate a gulf expedition, using Vera Cruz as a base for a march on Mexico City. With his own army idle, Taylor was to send every man he could spare for the new front. After landing at Vera Cruz in March 1847, General Scott's army occupied Mexico City on September 14. The invasion route took him through broken, mountainous terrain and a succession of gorges, peaks, passes, and forests. Once he took the Mexican capital, Scott faced a new threat from the rear after Mexican bandits and guerrillas began to plunder and cut his supply line to the coast. On October 6, Secretary of War Marcy ordered Scott to destroy all guerrilla headquarters, but his inexperienced troops proved to be no match for these raiders, and he lost communication with Vera Cruz.

On July 6, 1847, Jack Hays was named commander of the Texas frontier. Two days later he was ordered to take that portion of his command not needed on the frontier and report to the idle General Taylor at Mier. This time he was to recruit twelve-month men for the First Regiment, Texas Mounted Volunteers. After assigning two companies to Lt. Col. Peter H. Bell and leaving him in charge of the frontier, Hays took five companies and started for Mier on August 12, 1847. One day later, his regiment was transferred to the beleaguered Scott at the express order of President Polk, who wanted these Rangers to "disperse the guerrillas which infest the line between Vera Cruz and the interior of Mexico."

On August 21, this second regiment of Hays made camp twenty miles below Matamoros at Ranchita. Many of these men were raw recruits, so there were some early morale and discipline problems. Jack's adjutant, John S. "Rip" Ford, and Company E were sent as an advance element to secure a campsite at Vera Cruz. Ford chose Vergara, three miles from the coastal port and on the Jalapa road, and all five Ranger companies were there by October 17. Since Hays was the only field officer in the regiment, the men elected Capt. A. M. Truett as major.

While encamped at Vergara, each of Jack's 580 Rangers received two of the new Walker Colt long-barreled six-shooters. After two weeks of training and target practice, they were deadly proficient with the new weapon. Since Hays was among the most renowned military leaders in Mexico, many high-ranking army and navy officers sought to meet him. When he passed by tents of troops from other states, they would rush out and shout, "Hurray for Colonel Hays!"

The Texans were assigned to the same brigade as Gen. Caleb Cushing's Massachusetts regiment camped to their right. Hays was often in the saddle leading scouts. While he was gone, his tent orderly, John Buchanan, held open house for the New Englanders and shared with them a half barrel of fine whiskey that had been given to Jack. One day the Massachusetts sergeant of the guard visited Buchanan and started to walk out with an item that caught his fancy. Suddenly, a small, plainly dressed man appeared and said, "Put that down, sir!" After cursing and threatening to arrest the fellow, the sergeant stepped out of the tent to call a guard detail. At this point a boiling Rip Ford roared, "What! Put our colonel in the guardhouse. Don't you try it!" An even angrier Hays shouted, "Ford, order a file of men here." When the surprised sergeant learned he had been dressing down Colonel Hays, he expected to be court-martialed. Instead, he was detained for two days, then released with no charges made against him. Needless to say, he never dropped in on Buchanan again.

On November 2, 1847, Hays's Rangers were ordered to march and report to General Scott. The cocky Texans were spoiling for a fight and wanted to travel light and alone, but their prudent leader decided to march as escorts of Maj. Gen. Robert Patterson's division. Two days later, the total force of over 3,000 reached Jalapa, where a *New Orleans Picayune* correspondent noted, "The presence of Col. Hays and his . . . Texas Rangers acts like a charm upon the rascals [guerrillas]." By this time there were also American military governors and garrisons in occupied Puebla and Perote, and the war had moved from a conventional to a guerrilla phase; in fact, Mexican governmental policy called for the people to rise up and attack the American invaders within eight miles of occupied points.

Jack and two of his Ranger companies rode on to Puebla to join Brig. Gen. Joseph "Jo" Lane. Since curious Mexican residents were thronging the streets, some of the Texans decided to show off around the main plaza. As they galloped by, they jumped off and on their mounts and picked handkerchiefs and sticks off the ground. One Ranger even dashed by standing in his saddle, waving his six-shooters. One member of General Lane's brigade, Lt. Albert Brackett of the Fourth Regiment of Indiana Volunteers, watched them pass along the main street and observed:

They certainly were an odd-looking set of fellows, and it seems to be their aim to dress as outlandishly as possible . . . a thorough coating of dust over all, and covering their huge beards gave them a savage appearance . . . Each man carried a rifle, a pair of pistols, and . . . two of Colt's revolvers; a hundred of them could discharge a thousand shots in two minutes, and with what precision the Mexican alone can tell. I . . . could distinguish no difference between the officers and men. They carried no sabers.

When Lane and Hays decided to attack Mexican troops at Izucar de Matamoros, Jack took 135 Rangers on the expedition. The combined force killed sixty Mexicans and rescued twenty-one American prisoners, who were mounted on Mexican ponies and returned to service. The next day they began the return trip to Puebla with a train of captured ordnance.

Upon reaching a dangerous mountain pass called Galazara, an advance company of Rangers was suddenly attacked by 200 Mexican lancers. Jack ordered a charge by Capt. Jacob Roberts's company, which chased the enemy across a prairie, up a mountain slope, and over its crest. At this point another 500 Mexican lancers spilled out of a ravine. With their guns empty, Hays ordered his Rangers back to the main force while he singlehandedly covered their retreat. The whole enemy line opened fire and charged Jack, who would stop at intervals to shoot the closest pursuer.

Once the Rangers reached the head of General Lane's column, the two leaders rallied their men, counterattacked General Rea's lancers, and drove them from the field. The round trip of 120 miles included two days of hard fighting. In a report at Puebla, dated December 1, 1847, General Lane noted, "Never did any officer act with more gallantry than Colonel Hays in this affair . . . When he found it necessary to retire for the purpose of reloading, . . . he halted in their rear and, as the enemy advanced, deliberately shot two of them dead, and covered his [own] retreat."

Upon their return to Puebla, Jack and his Rangers were ordered on to Mexico City, and his five companies led Patterson's command into the capital on December 6, 1847. The impressed Gen. Ethan Allen Hitchcock wrote,

> Hays's Rangers have come, their appearance never to be forgotten. Not in any sort of uniform, but well mounted and doubly well armed: ... All sorts of coats, blankets, and head-gear, but they are strong athletic fellows. The Mexicans are terribly afraid of them.

Adjutant Rip Ford later recalled,

> Our entrance into the City of Mexico produced a sensation among the inhabitants. They thronged the streets along which we passed. The greatest curiosity prevailed to get a sight at "Los Diablos Tejanos" — the Texas Devils. When the Rangers arrived, many Americans were being killed within the city, but now men had come who took eye for eye, tooth for tooth ...

Trouble was not long in coming. Once Colonel Hays halted his men in the Grand Plaza opposite the cathedral, a hungry Ranger motioned to a Mexican with a basket of candy on his head. When the vendor came near, the Texan grabbed three handfuls of his wares. Thinking that he was being robbed, the Mexican threw a pebble at the Ranger, who killed him with one pistol shot. According to Ford, the Ranger intended to pay for the candy, knowing that Hays would not tolerate thievery. This unfortunate incident caused a frantic stampede among the crowd of 10,000 gathered on the plaza.

That very night, some Rangers were about to enter a local theater when a thief grabbed one of their handkerchiefs and ran. When he ignored an order in Spanish to stop, the Mexican was shot dead, and the Ranger victim coolly replaced his prized neckwear as if nothing had happened. From then on, the Texans pinned handkerchiefs in their pockets when walking the streets; the unlucky thief who tried to grab one received a sound beating.

Some of the Rangers stayed at the Inn of the National Theater while in the capital. One evening a party of them were ushered into the dining room, prompting a curious waiter to ask where they were from. When told that the guests were from Texas, the waiter dropped his tray and ran from the room.

When Gen. Winfield Scott learned of the two Mexicans being killed by Rangers, he called in Colonel Hays and said he would not be disgraced by such outrages. His dander up, Jack retorted that his men were not accustomed to being insulted without resenting it, and that he was willing to be held responsible for the killings. Such a strong stand served to convince the general that the Ranger actions were justified, and the offenders were not punished.

While Mexico City was under U.S. military occupation, three to five American soldiers were murdered in the streets each night, usually stabbed when they were drunk. One afternoon Ranger Adam Allsens wandered alone into a particularly dangerous part of the city called "Cutthroat." He was attacked by a Mexican mob and literally cut to pieces; his heart could be seen beating when Adam finally escaped on his horse. He held on to a flicker of life for eight hours, long enough for him to describe both the location and his assailants. Allsens was buried with military honors the next day as his outfit, Capt. Jacob Roberts's company, grieved in silence.

It soon became apparent that Adam's friends were planning a bloody vengeance. One night about 10:00, Colonel Hays heard shots while in his headquarters at No. 26 Doncella Street. His companion, Capt. P. W. Humphreys, thought it sounded like a barrage of six-shooter fire, but Jack assured him that a company of horse marines drilling outside the walls was responsible for the commotion. When Hays left the building at midnight, the firing suddenly stopped. During this two-hour period, the avenging Ranger company killed more than eighty Mexicans and left their bodies in the streets. It seems that the

U.S. Military Patrol also heard the firing, rushed to the scene, and joined in the killing rampage.

After a month of such bloody deeds, General Scott decided it would be best to occupy the Rangers with chasing guerrillas outside the city. On January 10, 1848, Colonel Hays took sixty-five men and went looking for the guerrilla-assassin leader, Padre Celedonia de Jarauta. After being informed that the priest was at San Juan Teotihuacán, Jack's Rangers occupied a large stone building on one side of the large town plaza. Most of the bone-tired Texans fell asleep, only to be awakened by shots and a combined infantry-cavalry attack. As 400 guerrillas opened fire from rooftops around the square, Jarauta led a mounted charge by seventy-five lancers. Luckily for the slumbering Rangers, Capt. Ephraim Daggett and five others stood in the door and heroically turned back the initial attack. While Hays ordered some Rangers to the top of the building, others rushed out into the square with six-shooters blazing. When Jarauta led another mounted charge with sword in hand, he was wounded, and the battle ended with the *padre* being carried off by his own men. The Mexicans suffered fifteen killed and five wounded, while Jack's troops had no injuries whatsoever. In less than thirty hours, his men had marched 107 miles and beaten an enemy force five times their size.

On January 18, Hays and four Ranger companies were assigned to General Lane for a secret expedition, the task of clearing all roads and seeking out guerrillas at Puebla and Oaxaco. After hearing that General Santa Anna was at Tehuacan, the force stopped a showy coach accompanied by a dozen armed guards en route. Since the one passenger had an American safe-conduct pass, General Lane ordered Hays to let him go despite the colonel's fears that he would warn Santa Anna of their approach. After traveling all night at a steady gallop, the expedition reached Tehuacan at dawn and saw a white flag in the plaza. The courier had warned him at 2:00 in the morning, and Santa Anna had just departed.

The seventeen packed trunks Santa Anna left behind contained hundreds of dresses, which were later forwarded to his wife by the gallant Lane. In one trunk was an ornate cane with a pedestal of gold and an eagle-shaped head of diamonds, rubies, sapphires, and emeralds. At the Rangers' insistence the cane was given to their "Colonel Jack." When Maj. William H. Polk inspected the prize, however, he requested that it be sent to his brother, President Polk, with Hays responding, "I have no use for such an ornament. Take it, Major, and give it to the president, and say it is a present from the Texans."

During the twenty-three days that Lane's secret expedition was absent from Mexico City, a dozen cities submitted to their demands, and six American prisoners were rescued.

When it was reported that Padre Jarauta had relocated in the mountains northeast of Mexico City, General Lane was ordered to stop his raiding activities. On February 17, 1848, Lane left the capital with 250 of Hays's Rangers and 130 of Major Polk's Third Dragoons. By daybreak they could see their objective, Tulancingo, in a valley nine miles away. Hoping to surprise the priest, they made the distance in a run, only to find that Jarauta and Gen. Mariano Paredes had been gone for two days. The disappointed Major Polk did capture a man named Paredes, but it was the general's brother. On the second night of the scout, Lane's men camped in a narrow valley near the *hacienda* of a wealthy Mexican. While searching the premises, they found a barrel of superior Madeira wine in a room adjacent to the church. The rich owner said, "I implore you not to drink that wine. It is consecrated." Capt. Alex Hays, a West Pointer from Pennsylvania, retorted, "Then we will drink it for the love of God."

Learning that Jarauta was at Sequalteplan with 450 guerrillas, Hays led the expedition out at midnight on a forced march. Arriving at sunrise on February 25, the Rangers caught the Mexicans by total surprise and charged into the walled barracks area after Jack's horse knocked open the gate. Leaving Truett and Chevaille in charge, he took the four other companies and raced to the main plaza, where they charged a large barracks full of lancers and infantry. Although outnumbered two to one, the Rangers won a running fight in chasing the enemy over half a mile. Returning to the plaza, they were dismounted and reinforced the outnumbered Lane. The Texans forced the doors of the well-sheltered Mexicans, killing thirty of them before the battle became a siege.

When it was over, 120 guerrillas were dead and only five Rangers wounded, but a disappointed Hays learned that Jarauta had escaped from a large church fronting the main plaza just minutes before American troops arrived. The priest never recovered from this defeat, however, and posed no further threat to U.S. occupation forces. When the Rangers started back to Mexico City on February 26, each carried a Mexican lance as a souvenir of their victory. In all, Lane's expedition lasted fourteen days and covered more than 500 miles. It should be noted that during a six-week period in which the Rangers were supposedly "quartered" in or near Mexico City, they were out marching or fighting for five of them.

After the armistice was ratified on March 4, 1848, Hays's Rangers were ordered to move down the Vera Cruz road, patrol it, and protect wagon trains. On April 20, General Lane's entire command marched out of Mexico City en route to the coast. Halfway between the capital and Puebla, Jack's regiment camped at the Rio Frio. His hostler was a young man who took care of fresh mounts for the colonel. The youth had the bad habit of loitering behind the column. At dawn his mutilated body was found in the road after the Rangers broke camp. The guerrillas who killed him also took two of the colonel's best horses.

During the march to the coast, Jack learned that

there was a guerrilla band sixteen miles away at San Juan de los Llanos. After detailing Rip Ford and fourteen Rangers to a scout, they arrived there at dusk to confront 4,000 celebrating a Saint's day in the town plaza. Ford demanded that the prefect of police provide quarters and provisions for his men. A large stone building was assigned the Rangers, but the prefect refused to furnish rations, saying that he had earlier been imposed upon by U.S. army deserters. At this point Rip identified himself as being in the Hays regiment, prompting the recalcitrant official to have a sudden change of heart. Rations were immediately furnished to "Devil Jack's" men, while Ford and his friends were treated to a sixteen-course dinner served on fine silver.

After the armistice, both Mexico and the United States gave permission for Santa Anna to leave the country. Fearing that he might still be taken prisoner, the general asked Col. George W. Hughes, the governor of occupied Jalapa, for safeguard to his estate near El Encero. On March 28, Hughes left Jalapa with an escort of three companies of Maryland mounted volunteers to meet Santa Anna at San Miguel, where a dinner was to be hosted by Gen. José Duran. Since Hays's Rangers were camped only four miles away, Hughes invited Jack to come and pay his respects to the defeated leader.

After much food and wine, Santa Anna began to make merry and grow boisterous, thoroughly enjoying the impression he was making on the Americans. Noticing Colonel Hays quietly standing in the crowd near the door, the escort commander, Maj. John R. Kenly, led him toward the dinner table to be presented to the famed Mexican leader. Suddenly, the Mexican escort officers began to stir and there was total silence. When Kenly said, "General, permit me to present to you Colonel Jack Hays," Santa Anna's countenance and demeanor changed and his wife turned very pale. After starting to rise, the general suddenly sat down and fixed his gaze on the table, even as Jack bowed politely and left the room.

Soon thereafter, Santa Anna informed Kenly that he was ready to march.

Hays's regiment was camped along both sides of the road between San Miguel and Jalapa, the route that Santa Anna would take in traveling to the coast. When Major Truett and Adjutant Ford rode to Jalapa to watch the Mexicans receive their foremost general, some Rangers rode from camp and told them, "The men say they are going to kill Santa Anna when he reaches there." The two officers hurried back to find the angry camp bent on revenge. Ford persuaded the Rangers not to assassinate Santa Anna by appealing to their honor and reason. When he said that such an act would "dishonor Texas," the men answered, "Then we will not do it."

Soon Major Kenly appeared, leading the American escort column. Behind them was the eight-mule open carriage carrying Santa Anna, his pretty second wife, and fifteen-year-old daughter. Hundreds of Rangers silently sat on stone fences on both sides of the road as the entourage passed by. According to Ford, the general sat erect and motionless, but "the old warrior's face blanched a little at the sight of his enemies of long standing." Even when the alarmed Mexicans drove the carriage teams into full speed, there were no disrespectful remarks from the Texans. Once the column was past, the Rangers broke ranks and returned to camp, where a proud Colonel Hays commended both officers and men for their conduct. It was Jack and a company of his Rangers who escorted Santa Anna from his El Encero estate to the coast, where he embarked on a Spanish ship bound for Venezuela on April 4, 1848.

While his regiment camped at El Encero, Hays went to Vera Cruz on April 10 to apply for transportation to Texas. His men had performed their final assignment well; the stage was now running between Puebla and Mexico City. While waiting to be mustered out, the Rangers conducted trials and found that the latest Colt six-shooter threw a ball farther than a Mississippi rifle could. The regiment also found time to remember their chaplain, Presbyterian minister Samuel H. Corley, who had acted as nurse, counselor, preacher, and provided words of cheer and comfort. As a memento of their respect and love, these rough-and-ready Rangers gave Reverend Corley $500 in gold. In a letter to Rip Ford, he later remarked, "God bless Hays's regiment; but for them I could never have paid my debts."

The last troops ordered to Vera Cruz, Jack's men finally camped at Vergara on April 29, 1848. All were mustered out of the service there except Hays and Ford, who were to rejoin the Ranger frontier guard in Texas. Rip later wrote that another brigadier general would have been appointed if the Mexican War had lasted longer, and that it was understood in Mexico City that Jack would have been the choice.

Sailing on the steamboat *Maria Burt,* the colonel and his officers landed at Powder Horn on Lavaca Bay, where a cannon salute, dinner, and ball awaited these Texas heroes. Since his clothes were too tattered and grimy for such festivities, Jack appeared in Santa Anna's padded fifteen-pound regimental coat. Valued at $1,000, it was made of coarse blue cloth with black and white satin trim. When Hays and his men reached Salado Creek, they were greeted by a delegation of San Antonio citizens. On May 20, 1848, a congratulatory ball for the returning Rangers attracted a crowd of over 300. A *New Orleans Picayune* correspondent noted that "the beautiful and amiable lady of Colonel Hays was the bright and particular star of the evening, . . . and the constant recipient of the most marked attention."

The most popular man in Texas, Jack soon surprised those who assumed he had political ambitions. On June 10, the *Austin Democrat* announced that he was retiring from the Ranger service due to "circumstances of a private nature," news which inspired the *Picayune* to carry a long, laudatory story about the "Retirement of Col. Hays."

By 1848, San Antonio businessmen were wanting to

establish trade with El Paso and Chihuahua, Mexico. This valuable business from Santa Fe to the northern states of Mexico had been going to Missouri, but they dreamed of diverting it for Texas. Knowing that Jack wanted to resume surveying, some San Antonio citizens approached him within days of his retirement and asked if he would explore and find the best wagon route to Chihuahua by way of the Paso del Norte. Hays expressed an interest in the project and was chosen to lead the "Chihuahua-El Paso Pioneer Expedition."

When he traveled to Washington in June to resign from the army, he was authorized to explore both a lower and upper route for a San Antonio-El Paso wagon road. His seventy-two-man expedition included thirty-five citizens from San Antonio and Fredericksburg, thirty-five Texas Rangers, and two guide-interpreters. Hays led the citizens, dividing them into parties of four with thirty days' rations and one pack mule each, and hired a Mexican guide named Lorenzo. His friend, Samuel Maverick, was despondent and haggard-looking over the recent death of a child, and Jack thought the trip would be a good tonic for him. When Samuel's wife agreed and persuaded him to go, Maverick was assigned to keep a log and diary of the expedition.

Hays and his group left San Antonio on August 27, 1848, and headed for a Ranger camp on the Llano near Castell. There they joined Capt. Samuel Highsmith, his thirty-five Rangers, and their interpreter, a Delaware chief named John Conner. On September 4, Hays led the combined force up the Llano to Comanche Creek, then followed the James River and north fork of the Nueces to Las Moras, a tributary of the Rio Grande. Heading west, the expedition reached what friendly Indians called the Puerce, a wide river bordered by cliffs and gorges that Jack named "Devil's River." Leading their horses on foot, his force reached the Pecos on September 26. They had traveled only 418 miles in a month, and the worst was yet to come.

The next day Delaware scout Jack Hunter noticed a small herd of buffalo bulls some three miles away. The hungry men made camp and sent out Hunter and Lorenzo, who had boasted of their endurance and fleetness of foot, along with Hays. Carrying a rifle, each man started off on an "Indian trot," but after ten minutes of running in the soft, flaky limestone, Hunter and Lorenzo slowed to a bare run. Within a few hundred yards of their game, both dropped totally exhausted. They could only watch sheepishly as Jack ran on at an effortless pace; loading as he ran, their leader killed three of the buffalo, then returned to camp and sent Maj. John Caperton to bring in the meat.

Lorenzo did not know the country west of the Pecos, so Hays took over as expedition guide. As they wandered through high, broken mountains, their food ran out and water became scarce. By October 6, Samuel Maverick noted that they were "eating mustang meat" which was "in great request." Some Mescalero Apaches then directed the expedition southwest toward San Carlos, a Mexican village on the south side of the Rio Grande. When they arrived there on October 18, the group had been out of rations for twelve days and had been eating grass, rattlesnakes, skunks, panthers, and pack mules. While camping near San Carlos, Hays's men purchased enough food to reach Fort Leaton, then headed upriver and reached Presidio del Norte on the twenty-second. The expedition then went to Fort Leaton, a trading post and ranch five miles away on the Texas side, where Ben Leaton sold them provisions and mules. Although El Paso was only 150 miles away over known terrain, winter was approaching. Hays decided to return home after resting sixteen days at Fort Leaton. Ben hosted a farewell barbecue when they left and persuaded Jack to take his small son to attend school at San Antonio.

On October 31, 1848, the expedition left Fort Leaton headed northeast, finding the 150 miles to the Pecos to be level country and good for year-round traveling. Reaching the head of Devil's River, Hays split his group into three parties: twenty-eight men went east and directly to San Antonio, Captain Highsmith traveled northeast to the Concho and his own Ranger camp, while Jack took thirteen men to explore the Las Moras River region to the southeast. Finding the area unpromising, Hays's party was back in San Antonio on December 10, concluding an expedition that traveled 1,303 miles in 106 days. In a detailed report to Secretary of War Marcy, he suggested that the best wagon road route from San Antonio ran north to the San Saba, then through Concho country to the Pecos, and west to El Paso. His expedition had discovered a new, practicable route to tap the Chihuahua-Santa Fe trade for Texas.

While Hays was off exploring the Big Bend area, he was appointed district surveyor for the Bexar District by Governor George T. Wood. He showed no interest when Austin supporters pressured him to announce for governor in January 1849. Two months later, the U.S. Congress created the Department of the Interior with Indian affairs under its jurisdiction. On April 11, 1849, the Office of Indian Affairs named Hays as Indian sub-agent for the newly acquired Gila River country.

In only thirteen years in Texas, Jack had won fame as a Ranger leader and Indian fighter. When he left San Antonio to begin his new job in early June 1849, he was embarking on a new career as a builder of the San Francisco Bay area. Frontier service to Texas had made him a legendary figure, but wealth and social-political standing awaited him in California.

Traveling with Maj. John Caperton and forty men, Hays accompanied a detachment of army engineers and infantry escort building the road to El Paso. Ironically, General Harney ignored Jack's suggestion to take a northern, upper route, and instead ordered the engineers to take the Woll road west of San Antonio, then follow a lower route. While camped opposite old El Paso for almost five weeks, Hays concluded that he could not make a treaty with the treacherous, warlike Gila Apaches. He

78

became convinced that these Indians would have to be severely chastised and made to fear the United States before they would accept reservation life. Seeing that an adequate reservation policy would be years in coming, Jack decided to resign his post while he was in Tucson. There he agreed to lead a small party of emigrants through Apache country to California. Taking a new route through the desert, he led his group thirty miles a day down the Gila River to the Colorado, reached the California side on December 5, 1849, and was in San Diego by the end of the month.

After officially resigning his post as Indian sub-agent, Hays took the brig, *Colonel Fremont,* on a stormy voyage to San Francisco in mid-January 1850. Shortly after arriving there on January 25, he wrote Susan in San Antonio and observed, "What a future for commerce!" A San Francisco newspaper had already announced the coming of "Colonel Jack Hays," prompting a committee of local businessmen to approach the "celebrated Texas Ranger" and ask if he would run for sheriff of San Francisco County. Short of funds and needing a job, Jack agreed to run as an independent candidate against the Democratic nominee, "Colonel" J. J. Bryant, a gambler and faro dealer who lavished $50,000 in barroom food and drink during the campaign. On election day, April 1, 1850, Bryant's manager staged an impressive noontime parade on the plaza. Shortly thereafter, Hays rode into view on a spirited black stallion and put on a daring display of fine horsemanship. A host of impressed "city slickers" rushed to vote for the famed Ranger, and the "people's choice" took office on April 9, with John Caperton as undersheriff.

Controlling a boomtown of 40,000 taxed even Hays's energy, and the sheriff soon moved from the Adelphi House to the Marine Hospital to get more rest. He was aided by a volunteer 200-man night patrol, the "Committee of Vigilance of San Francisco." Their first prisoner, John Jenkins, was hanged on the plaza for stealing a safe. These vigilantes boasted that Sheriff Hays was with them "Heart and Soul" and helped raise money for a better jail with Jack using prisoners to build it. During his term, the California legislature leased state prisoners for ten years to two contractors, who agreed to guard and maintain them in return for their labor. Hays and Caperton then subleased the contract, using seventy of the prisoners in a rock quarry and for cutting and grading the streets of San Francisco. After only four months, however, the sheriff halted the program as he began losing money on it. Jack also helped organize the city's first volunteer fire department, the Monumental Fire Company.

In late September 1850, Mrs. Hays left San Antonio to join her husband. Accompanied by Jack's brother Bob, Susan traveled by ship by way of Panama and reached San Francisco in early December. After being reunited with his wife, Hays purchased the Mountain Home Ranch, a 2,000-acre spread thirty miles down the peninsula, and rode to work each day. When he was reelected sheriff over Whig Charles M. Elleard in September 1851, Jack and Susan moved to a house in the city on Powell Street. On August 25, 1852, Susan had their first child, John Caperton Hays. Remembering a promise made years ago in Texas, his proud father nick-named him "Buffalo Hump, Jr." Upon hearing of the birth, the Comanche war chief sent the baby a fine gold goblet and two gold spoons.

Among Hays's early acquaintances in San Francisco were the four Peralta brothers, sons of Luis Peralta, who had received a Spanish land grant of ten square leagues which embraced two oak-covered peninsulas or *encinals*. In March 1852, Hays and Caperton put up one-fourth of the $10,000 purchase price in buying Vicente Peralta's *encinal*. Vicente had been having trouble keeping squatters off this land on which present Oakland stands. The purchase made Jack a wealthy man and a founder of the city.

During the presidential campaign of 1852, Sheriff

Hays served as vice-president of the Granite Club, which helped Franklin Pierce carry California and win the election. Hoping to be appointed federal surveyor general for California, Jack took a four-month leave of absence as sheriff to attend the Pierce inauguration, sailing from California on January 15, 1853. The two were warm friends, and Pierce had served as a brigadier general in the Mexican War. After getting the appointment at Washington, Hays attended the president's reception, where he was surrounded by admirers and curious guests. One of them observed that there was danger that "the Colonel was going to steal the show." He then made a short visit to Richmond, Virginia, to pay his respects to the mother of a dear friend and comrade in arms, the late Major Chevaille.

A reporter for the *Richmond Examiner* found it difficult to reconcile Jack's extraordinary accomplishments with his ordinary appearance. In devoting several columns to Hays's visit, the article noted:

> Amid the countless multitude attracted to Washington ... during the last few weeks ... no man was the object of deeper interest than Col. Jack Hays, the world renowned Texan ranger ... It may be safely asserted that no man in America, since the great John Smith explored the primeval forests of Virginia ... has run a career of such boldness, daring and adventure. His frontier defense of the Texas Republic constitutes one of the most remarkable pages in the history of the American character. For importance of results, brought about by apparently utterly inadequate means, his services stand preeminent — for daring and endurance, for privation, suffering, and hard fighting, this soldier with his little band of followers stands without a parallel scarcely in the history of warfare ...

Before returning to San Francisco, Jack visited New Orleans and spent a few days at San Antonio, where he "engendered quite a California fever."

Four days after his return, Hays resigned as sheriff

after holding that job more than three years. Although he served during a particularly corrupt period, Jack was above reproach and maintained a reputation for honesty. Two observers attest to his efficiency: An editor said that "He was almost the only man in San Francisco who could quell a disturbance," while a contemporary, J. P. Allsopp, later noted, "Jack was, in his day, a terror to evil doers."

On July 16, 1853, Hays took office as surveyor general of California with headquarters on Kearny Street in San Francisco. The next year he and Susan moved to Oakland. If he happened to miss the ferryboat, Jack often took on the tides and winds in rowing himself across the bay to work. The outdoors always beckoned him, and he was soon a leader of the Coast Rangers, a hunting club that went on annual excursions. Starting in May 1855, he was the first to survey public lands on the eastern slope of the Sierras. In December 1857, Hays traveled to Washington to confer with the land commissioner about the deficiency in his deputies' accounts, some $175,000 in survey contracts which exceeded the legal appropriations. The controversy ended with Congress voting to pay the deficiency and a San Francisco newspaper saying of Jack, "Of all men in California, he occupies the proudest and most distinguished position."

Between 1853 and 1866, Hays became a wealthy man by selling off downtown lots in Oakland. The land he and Caperton owned on the waterfront was valued at an average of $3,000 an acre, and Jack was once offered $300,000 for some of this acreage. In November 1857, he sold sixty acres of land which became the site of the University of California. In February 1869, he contracted with university regents to locate its agricultural college lands. In 1858 he led eight local businessmen in a vain effort to persuade the legislature to move the state capital to Oakland. Jack and his friends offered to give twenty acres of city land as a building site and to provide "a temporary state house" and other buildings, with Hays putting up collateral of $20,000.

Because of new President James Buchanan's commitment to the rotation-in-office principle, Hays was appointed surveyor general of Utah Territory in July 1857, and confirmed by the U.S. Senate the following April. Although he was thankful that the appointment had "wiped away everything like an imputation upon my character," Jack never went to Utah or drew a salary. In February 1859, he resigned the post because the illness of a child prevented him from taking his family there.

In the late autumn of 1859, Jack and Susan moved to Fernwood, an 800-acre ranch just outside Oakland and near Piedmont in Alameda County. He macadamized the road to the ranch, and the grounds included extensive lawns and gardens, graveled walks, and hundreds of trees and shrubs. It was here that the couple raised a surviving son and daughter, John C. and Elizabeth; four other Hays children died in infancy. Susan Hays was an accomplished horsewoman and loved to ride about Fernwood with her husband. Jack was a graceful dancer and gracious host; it was not uncommon for 100 guests to attend their Sunday morning breakfasts. He was also a doting chaperon when his pretty and charming Betty threw parties at the ranch. When John Caperton Hays married Anna McMullin in November 1880, some 1,500 invitations went out for one of the most brilliant social events of the San Francisco season.

Jack led his final campaign against the Indians while living in California. After the discovery of the Comstock Lode, miners rushed to Virginia City, Nevada. This mass intrusion by Californians triggered an uprising by the Paiute Indians in the spring of 1860. In May they massacred Maj. William Ormsby and forty-six volunteers sent to punish them for a raid on Williams's Station. At this time Colonel Hays arrived in Carson Valley "on private business." Legend has it that he came to help an old comrade in arms, Texas Ranger Capt. Edward Storey, who had raised the Virginia City Rifles to fight the Paiutes. On May 24, Jack agreed to take command of the volunteer Washoe Regiment, subject to the condition that he exercise absolute control and discipline over these 530 volunteers, many of whom had been Indian fighters in Texas. When they were joined by Captain Steward's 212 federal troops from Carson City, Hays was put in command of both forces.

Following a desert march to the Truckee River, Jack's men encountered the Paiutes at Pinnacle Mount on June 2, 1860. During three hours of hand-to-hand fighting, 200 volunteers and 100 regulars drove between 800 and 1,000 Indians from their hiding places, then chased them four miles before the Paiutes fled to their mountain retreat. Although Chief Winnemucca escaped, his power was broken and an army detachment was subsequently able to contain his tribe. After only ten days of service, Colonel Hays was able to disband the volunteers while the grateful people of Nevada presented him with a handsome silver service and a beautiful black horse for his wife.

As the years went by, Jack played a key role in the development of Oakland. He was a major stockholder in the Oakland Gas Light Company and a founder and director of the Union National Bank and the Union Savings Bank. Hays gave the city acreage for three parks, donated several building sites for churches, and sold seventy-five acres to the Ocean View School District for a mere $100. In 1877, he was assessed at $162,700 for local property taxes; that September his agent for Alameda property advertised sixty-four lots. By this time he had purchased almost 10,000 acres of state land and had an estate of more than a half million dollars.

In his twilight years Hays was active in state Democratic politics. As a delegate to the 1876 national convention at St. Louis, he placed in nomination the name of Samuel J. Tilden. He also found time to serve as a director of the state school for the deaf, dumb, and blind. When he rode into Oakland on horseback, this modest old hero felt uncomfortable when the curious rushed to the sidewalk edge to catch a glimpse of "Colonel Jack, the

Ranger." To avoid such attention he resorted to a buggy for transportation.

In 1879 and 1880, the retired capitalist spent his winters in Arizona and San Diego, respectively, seeking relief from attacks of rheumatism. When he became seriously ill, Jack started to assign his property to his wife and son, eventually leaving only $10,000 of property in his own name. Failing health left him stooped, in much pain, and unable to visit his friends. After spending the winter of 1882 in an Oakland hotel for the convenience of his physician, Hays returned to the ranch the following spring.

Shortly after 1:00 P.M. on April 21, 1883, the sixty-six-year-old warrior suffered an internal hemorrhage, and the alarmed family sent for Dr. I. D. Nicholson. About 3:30 that afternoon, Jack looked up at John Freaner, his longtime friend and former first deputy, and cheerfully asked, "John, do you know what day this is?" When told that it was Saturday, the old Ranger replied, "Yes, John, and it's San Jacinto Day!" He then closed his eyes, lost consciousness, and died minutes later.

When the San Francisco *Morning Call* printed a story about the death of Jack Hays, it was titled "A Hero Gone." The family wanted a simple home ceremony, but the citizens of Oakland insisted on a "partial military funeral," the most elaborate the city had seen. After the body lay in state in the south parlor at Fernwood, the funeral procession went down Broadway to St. John's Episcopal Church. Once the service was completed, the Oakland Light Cavalry served as escort and honor guard in carrying the body of Hays to Mountain View Cemetery.

To this writer the words of the Apostle Paul (II Timothy 4:7) provide a fitting epitaph for Colonel Jack Hays: "I have fought a good fight, I have finished my course, I have kept the faith."

Captain John Coffee (Jack) Hays, 1844 photograph.

— Courtesy Perry-Castañeda Library, The University of Texas at Austin

John Coffee Hays in later years.

— Courtesy Institute of Texan Cultures, San Antonio, Texas Source: Library of Congress

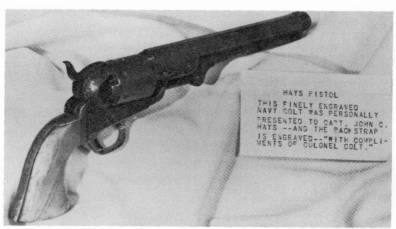

Jack Hays's 1851 Navy Colt revolver, a gift from Col. Samuel Colt.

— Courtesy Texas Ranger Museum, Waco, Texas

86

Hays's Texas Rangers, 1844. Hays stands in front in white shirt sleeves.
— Courtesy Perry-Castañeda Library,
The University of Texas at Austin

87

Sam Maverick

— Courtesy Texas State
Library, Archives
Division,
Austin, Texas

Col. John S. (Rip) Ford

— Courtesy Texas State
Library, Archives
Division,
Austin, Texas

Enchanted Rock

— Courtesy Awani Press, Fredericksburg, Texas
Photo by Douglass Hubbard

88

III

Richard King:
Founder of a Ranching Empire

Richard King came to Texas with his belongings in a seabag and made his first fortune steamboating on the Rio Grande. A greater vision led him to buy, settle on, and defend land where the original Mexican owners dared not live. By succeeding in this daring, dangerous venture, King brought civilization and peace to an empty wilderness where bloodshed and plunder had prevailed. Unlike some cattle barons of his day, he did not resort to force or duplicity in creating a ranching empire; the King ranges were acquired legally and purchased from willing sellers. A mutual sense of obligation and responsibility bound Captain King and his Mexican *vaqueros,* a tradition which is the bedrock of the King Ranch. This hard-drinking, brawling Irish frontiersman was devoted to — but never totally tamed by — the prim, proper daughter of a Presbyterian preacher. He sought to cultivate the image of a "man-eater," yet was an over-indulgent husband and father to his "pets." The captain died a millionaire, and his legacy is the most famous — and fabled — ranch in America.

The son of poor Irish immigrants, Richard was born in New York City on July 10, 1824, but the family soon moved to Orange County, where the blue-eyed, black-haired sturdy lad spent his early years. According to family history, his parents died when Richard was only five and an aunt signed papers apprenticing him to a New York jeweler in return for his room and board when he was nine. Instead of learning a trade, however, young Richard served as a janitor and babysitter and so disliked his master that he ran away to the docks. He felt at home there among the roustabouts and proved to be an apt pupil in learning their job.

King was just eleven and had only a loaf of bread to his name when he stowed away on the sailing ship *Desdemona* in June 1835. Four days out of New York, he was discovered hiding in the cargo hold, but Richard persuaded the captain to make him a cabin boy rather than send him back. During the voyage to Mobile Bay, he was treated well and began to absorb the routine of life at sea. Upon reaching their destination, the skipper sent young King to a friend, Hugh Monroe, a steamboat captain whose shallow-draft boats plied the coastal rivers.

For the next two years, the earnest, square-jawed, high-spirited teenager worked on the river boats. He was taken in as a steamboat "cub" by Capt. Joe Holland, who made the Alabama River run from Mobile to Montgomery. In addition to learning equipment and the pilothouse, Richard was taught reading and arithmetic by Captain Holland. The skipper also arranged to send him to Connecticut, where two of Holland's elderly sisters enrolled the "cub" in eight months of real school, King's only formal education.

Leaving the Hollands and school behind, Richard signed on for steamboat service in Florida during the Seminole War. During 1841 and 1842, the brawny riverman worked boats in Tampa Bay and on the Apalachicola and Chattahoochee rivers. King had his pilot's license by 1843, when he met a solemn, prim Quaker named Mifflin Kenedy, the master of the steamboat *Champion*. The studious, reflective Kenedy was a native of Downington, Pennsylvania, and a former teacher, sailor, and brickyard worker. This powerful master could throw a huge anchor overboard by himself and seemed to complement the rowdy, profane King, who was seven years his junior but just as hardy and ambitious.

In the spring of 1846, Kenedy took the *Champion* up the Mississippi and Ohio to Pittsburgh for a general overhaul. There he met Capt. John Sanders, U.S. Army Engineers, whose assignment was to procure vessels to carry General Zachary Taylor's men and supplies on the Rio Grande during the Mexican War. The army was in dire need of experts who could handle shallow-draft riverboats, and Mifflin informed his friend Richard of that fact by letter. On July 2, 1846, Kenedy sailed on the steamer *Corvette* for New Orleans with his master's certificate in hand. After the vessel was purchased there for government service, Captain Kenedy arrived at the mouth of the Rio Grande in late August and wrote King again, saying that he was needed in Texas. By then the United States Army had occupied the Mexican towns of Matamoros, Camargo, and Mier. The following spring found Richard King in New Orleans, where he signed on as a steamboat pilot for the duration of the Mexican War.

With only a seabag in hand, the burly twenty-two-year-old King was put ashore by a dinghy near the mouth of the Rio Grande in May 1847. On the south side of the river, he could see a smuggler's haven called Bagdad, a trap where strangers could expect to lose their money by fair — or foul — play. While waiting for Kenedy, Richard stayed on the Texas side of the river at Boca del Rio, a shantytown for boatmen.

When the Irish steamboater first set foot on Texas soil, the area between the Nueces River and the Rio Grande was an empty wilderness labeled the Wild Horse Desert on one map. This country had been claimed by both the Republic of Texas and Mexico, and the bitter dispute was the major cause of the Mexican War. The lonely prairies and thickets of this Nueces Strip provided a haven for mustangers, outlaws, and remnants of the dreaded Karankawa Indians. Although Mexicans owned the land titles in this region, they dared not live there because of raiding Lipan and Comanche Indians.

After General Taylor won victories at Monterrey and Buena Vista, much of his army was reassigned to Gen. Winfield Scott for his assault on Mexico City. Although Taylor was left with only defensive operations, his army still had to be supplied in northern Mexico. On June 13, 1847, Second Pilot King reported for duty on the steamer *Colonel Cross*. Seventeen days later he was reassigned to the *Corvette,* serving as first pilot to his friend, Captain Kenedy. Between the southern tip of Padre Island and Brazos Santiago Island was a navigable channel and anchorage called Brazos Santiago, which served as the sea terminal for Taylor's army. It was there that the *Corvette* picked up New Orleans cargo from deeper-draft seagoing ships, then ferried the goods eight miles by open sea to the mouth of the Rio Grande and upriver as far as Camargo and Mier. The supplies were then carried overland by mule train to Taylor's troops.

In carrying out his assignment, First Pilot King kept the chart in his head for 250 miles of snaggy, crooked, and variable river to the head of navigation at Mier. (It should be noted that the distance *by road* from the sea to Mier was only 175 miles, the difference due to the twisting Rio Grande.) The *Corvette* was actually a deluxe steamboat built for passenger service on the Ohio River before the government paid $16,000 for her at Pittsburgh. Because of her superior accommodations, Commanding General Scott used the vessel on his one trip up the river to Camargo in January 1847. During all of her wartime service on the Rio Grande under Kenedy and King, the *Corvette* was kept running and in continuous operation without a single damaging accident.

The Mexican War ended when General Scott's army occupied Mexico City on September 14, 1847. By November, Richard King was captain of the *Colonel Cross,* the steamboat that carried General Taylor downriver from Camargo to Brazos Santiago, where he boarded a ship for New Orleans on November 26. A peace treaty was signed at Guadalupe Hidalgo on February 2, 1848, in which a defeated Mexico recognized the Rio Grande as the boundary of Texas. The war's end released Richard from government service, but he tarried on the river after learning that the Quartermaster Department was planning to sell as war surplus the small fleet of immobilized steamboats. While waiting to bid on a boat, he spent the last months of 1848 operating a flophouse at Boca del Rio, where he made beds, mixed drinks, and acted as bouncer.

During this time his pal Kenedy was representing Matamoros merchants in promoting the new town of Roma, located on a high stone bluff on the east bank of the Rio Grande. Situated halfway between Camargo and Mier, Roma could compete for the Mexican trade with the monopoly previously enjoyed by Henry Clay Davis at Rancho Davis (later Rio Grande City).

On December 6, 1848, the *American Flag* advertised that the public sale of eleven steamboats would take place on April 2, 1849. However, only six of the vessels were sold at very low prices due to a combination of factors: many Americans had left the lower Rio Grande after the war; river business had declined; a cholera epidemic had swept the region. King knew the condition of his boat, the *Colonel Cross,* and was able to purchase the vessel for only $750. Three years earlier, it had cost the federal government $14,000 at Pittsburgh.

Operating the *Colonel Cross* was no bonanza during that lean first year. Richard pulled duty as owner, master, and pilot, and hired only an engineer, cook, and a dozen Mexican stokers and deck hands. While carrying cargo from Matamoros merchants to Camargo and settlers in northeastern Mexico, King had occasion to visit with Kenedy at Roma. At that time Mifflin was trying to sell river real estate and operating merchandise pack mule trains to Zacatecas and Monterrey.

After the war, King's chief steamboat competitor was Charles "Carlos" Stillman, an American trader who had lived at Matamoros since 1828. Stillman had organized the Brownsville Town Company in December 1848, then hired a surveyor to lay out a townsite, sold town lots, and built a ferry service from the new town to Matamoros. In February 1850, Charles asked Mifflin Kenedy to be his partner and make his steamboats profitable. Kenedy gave his approval only after a reluctant Stillman agreed to also bring in King. The young Irishman proceeded to inform Charles that his old boats were not designed for their job: they were too light for the outside gulf run and too heavy for the inside Rio Grande run. If Stillman would bankroll the project, Richard would design two kinds of boats. A big, stout side-wheeler would carry large cargoes to a downriver terminal, where it would be transferred to a smaller, high-powered mudskimmer and taken upriver. According to King, the lowered cargo-handling costs would mean sure profits.

Once Stillman was sold on the concept, the new "common carrier" of M. Kenedy & Co. was created at Brownsville on March 1, 1850, with Charles's steamboater, James O'Donnell, as the fourth partner. Mifflin carried Richard's diagrams and specifications to Pittsburgh, placed a special order for two steamers, the *Grampus* and the *Comanche,* and was back on the Rio Grande by July. The rugged 1,500-ton *Grampus* was designed for short runs with its limited fuel spaces allowing more deck for cargoes. The 200-ton *Comanche,* on the other hand, was a powerful light "mudder" with a draft of less than twenty-four inches loaded.

During the spring and summer of 1850, King continued to operate the *Colonel Cross.* While making a run to Brownsville that February, he met the love of his life. He arrived there to find an old steamboat, the *Whiteville,* moored in and blocking his unloading slip; in fact, the cursing captain had to quickly back his engine to get around her. The *Whiteville* had been converted to a houseboat and was being rented by the new preacher in town, Reverend Hiram Chamberlain.[1] While Richard was raving and ranting about the rat-infested scow docked in *his* berth, a dainty, pretty seventeen-year-old lady suddenly appeared on the tidy gunwale of the house-boat and put him in his place with an indignant tongue-lashing before stalking out of sight. As soon as Kenedy came aboard, the smitten King casually inquired about the new preacher *and* his daughter, Henrietta Maria Morse Chamberlain. It seems that her father was in Brownsville to found a Presbyterian church and the Rio Grande Female Institute, where Henrietta was to teach.

Richard was anxious to meet this lass with the bright brown eyes and asked his friend Mifflin for a proper introduction. Kenedy agreed only if King would attend the Wednesday night prayer meeting and church social on board the *Whiteville*. The prospective suitor was more than willing to endure two such novel experiences and went back repeatedly after meeting Henrietta. From then on, the rough-and-tumble steamboater paid more attention to his parlor manners and always managed to tie up in Brownsville every Wednesday night so he could feast his eyes on Miss Chamberlain singing in the church choir. Although she was quick to reciprocate a romantic

---

[1] Hiram Chamberlain was a graduate of Middlebury College and two theological seminaries. While he was representing the Home Mission Society, Henrietta was born of his first wife, Maria Morse, at Boonville, Missouri, on July 21, 1832. At age fourteen, Henrietta was sent away for two years of schooling at the Female Institute at Holly Springs, Mississippi. When her letters revealed feelings of homesickness, her stern father admonished Henrietta that it was her "religious duty" to rise above that, deny herself, and sacrifice some happiness to improve her studies; she was to show some spirit and noble resolution, and "be a soldier for a few months." Reverend Chamberlain was twice a widower when he married Anna Adelia Griswold in October 1842. After feeling a mis-sionary calling to Texas, he waited until their youngest of three sons was old enough to travel, then struck out from Tennessee with the family in a coach and Hiram riding a mule. Finding no living quarters in Brownsville, he rented the *Whiteville* on the river.

interest, it took much longer for her stern father to accept young King; as granddaughter Alice later recalled, "*In time* Rev. Hiram Chamberlain grew to admire this young captain's sterling qualities and strong personality."

By August 1850, the *Grampus* and the *Comanche* were operating on the Rio Grande after arriving from Pittsburgh. Once they completed successful trial runs as the outside and inside boats, "outside man" King commanded the *Grampus,* the only steamer meeting schooners at Brazos Santiago. A transfer terminal was built ten miles upriver at the White Ranch, and "inside man" Kenedy took charge of river business as master of the *Comanche.* For his part, Charles Stillman was responsible for rounding up business.

The King system kept transshipments to a minimum and drove competitors from the river. By early 1852, M. Kenedy & Co. had a steamboat monopoly of water-borne goods into northeastern Mexico. In February of that year, the company contracted with the U.S. Army to transport military stores from Brazos Santiago to Fort Brown (Brownsville) and Ringgold Barracks. In the early 1850s, company headquarters moved from the Stillman Building in Brownsville to a new brick warehouse on the riverfront. By 1857, M. Kenedy & Co. was making annual profits of $40,000 and paying dividends of over fifty percent. Charles gradually became a silent partner, with Mifflin and Richard actually running the business and hiring others to handle their steamboats. The partners were unique for the times in that they did not smuggle goods into Mexico.

On April 16, 1852, Mifflin Kenedy married Petra Vela de Vidal of Mier, the twenty-six-year-old widow of a Mexican army colonel. The tall, attractive Petra and her five children settled down with her new husband at Brownsville. That spring his partner received an invitation from Henry Lawrence Kinney, a frontier smuggler, rogue, and the founder of Corpus Christi, to attend the Lone Star Fair there, a world's fair he was hosting. King readily accepted since the trip afforded an opportunity to see the country and check out a suggestion made by Texas Ranger Captain Gideon K. "Legs" Lewis.

The two had first met in 1851, when the Ranger company was being supplied by Richard's steamboat. Lewis had a fascinating proposal: that the two start a livestock venture by grazing the tall prairie grass on the deserted Wild Horse Desert. The curious King left Brownsville by horseback in late April 1852, taking the old 165-mile route called "General Taylor's Road" to Corpus Christi. Toward the end of the five-day trip, Richard noticed the good water and stirrup-high grass along Santa Gertrudis Creek, his first vision of a great ranch. To promoter Kinney, the Lone Star Fair was a bust: there were only 2,000 visitors, and his land and livestock sales were far short of expectations. To Richard King, however, the trip netted a potential bonanza: he found his friend, Legs Lewis, at the fair, and the two concluded a ranching partnership, starting with a cow camp on a creek. Upon his return to Brownsville, King told Kenedy:

> Land and livestock have a way of increasing in value. Cattle and horses, sheep and goats, will reproduce themselves into value. But boats — they have a way of wrecking, decaying, falling apart, decreasing in value and increasing in cost of operation.

Richard's first concern was finding some armed fighting men to protect the site of his proposed cow camp. Partner Lewis solved that problem by having himself appointed captain of a Ranger company charged with patrolling and protecting the Corpus Christi area from September 1852 until March 1853. During this period, King selected the most promising spot for a budding ranch, a site forty-five miles southwest of Corpus Christi near the springs that fed Santa Gertrudis Creek. His headquarters were in the forks formed by that creek and San Fernando Creek near their confluence with Baffin's Bay. Although Richard was supposed to be the absentee provider of funds, he chose to stay on and personally manage the cow camp.

The land where he squatted had originally been granted to Juan Mendiola of Camargo by the state of Tamaulipas in 1834. Juan had built a house and pens there before dying two years later, and his land was abandoned during the Texas Revolution. After tracking down Mendiola's heirs at Rio Grande City, King paid them $300 — less than two cents an acre — for their useless holdings on July 25, 1853. This tract of three and a half square Spanish leagues (15,500 acres), known as the Rincon de Santa Gertrudis grant, would become the nucleus of the fabled King Ranch and would later include the city of Kingsville. Before the deed was filed in Corpus Christi that November, Richard sold Lewis undivided half-interest in the tract for $2,000. Legs had purchased two tracts totaling seven leagues nearby and sold his partner half-interest for $1,000.

In late November 1853, King was one of five chain carriers for the surveyor of his land. In his memoirs, Ranger Rip Ford had this to say about Richard's commitment to hold on to his fortified cow camp:

> ... The men who held it were of no ordinary mould. They had come to stay. It was no easy matter to scare them ... They had determined to make a ranch on the Santa Gertrudis or leave their bones to tell of their failure.

On May 20, 1854, King and Lewis paid $1,800 for a much larger area due west of their original holdings, the de la Garza Santa Gertrudis grant. This tract of twelve square leagues (53,000 acres) was rectangular-shaped, with the creek flowing its entire length.

When a drought in 1853–54 reduced the flow of the Rio Grande, steamboater King was able to devote most of his time to his land and livestock. He first built a rough dirt dam across the bed of Tranquitas Creek, creating a tank that could water a thousand cattle. This dam was the first major capital improvement between Corpus Christi and Brownsville.

Richard's first cattle came from the border *ranchos* of Camargo and Mier. In his ranch account book, kept initially at Brownsville, the first entry for the purchase of cattle was dated January 12, 1854. In that transaction King paid Juan Cantu a total of $262.60 for forty-two cows delivered at Santa Gertrudis. On August 3, 1854, "King's Rancho" paid $200 for an American gray stallion and $300 for an American bay stallion; on November 28, another $600 was paid for one sorrel stud. During that first year, Richard paid out a total of $12,275.79, using all of his river cash as seed money for his budding ranch.

Once the Ranger patrol company was disbanded in March 1853, partners King and Lewis had to protect themselves. They started by hiring Capt. James Richardson, a gunman and veteran of the Mexican War, as chief guard and foreman in their absence. Surprise attacks were unlikely because they kept informants on alert to warn of raiders and hired private rangers to scout the territory. A prominent feature of the cow camp was a rough stockade and blockhouse with a mounted war surplus cannon from a King steamboat. A lookout was posted on top of the warehouse to scan the surrounding countryside. Richard took care to hire men for ranch work who could also fight, many of whom were Mexican friends who had served as his boat hands. Although he traveled with armed outriders as guards and was a "capital marksman" with a pistol, King was ambushed more than once.

The tradition of Los Kineños ("the King's men") dates from early 1854, when Richard traveled to a little village in Tamaulipas and persuaded their elders to move about one hundred Mexican men, women, and children to the Santa Gertrudis. The whole village came with all their possessions, and King promised to be their *Señor Capitan,* to build them homes, provide jobs, and pay wages in cash. The cowboys received food, twenty-five pesos a month, and lived with their families in *jacales,* wood-and-dirt huts with thatched roofs. These villagers who followed King en masse back to Texas were the beginnings of a special breed of *vaqueros.* From then on, English was the office language of "King's Rancho" but Spanish that of the open range. To this day, employment on the ranch is passed down through the generations; almost all of the present Kineños were born on the ranch and are descendants of the original crew of cowpunchers.[2]

After a four-year courtship, Richard married Henrietta Chamberlain on December 10, 1854. Her father performed the ceremony after the Sunday evening service of the First Presbyterian Church of Brownsville. King

---

[2] There is an almost feudal web of relationships on the ranch; it functions on the basis of inheritance of both property and position. One generation succeeds the next in every job, from *vaquero* to foreman to owner. Many *vaqueros* work their entire life on the ranch, raise their children there, and die on it. Only one tradition, the roundup, remains from the open-range days of their forefathers. While cattle are still worked in the open on horseback on the 238,000-acre Norias Division, they are worked in pens or gathered by helicopter on the other three divisions of the ranch.

The Kineños live in modest free housing and are provided free electricity, water, and milk. Each division has its own store, and the Laureles and Santa Gertrudis divisions provide schools. The average wage of a *vaquero* ranges from $12,000 to $15,000 a year. Because of their material well-being, the Kineños have shown no interest in unionization; in fact, a union organizer has said, "If we could get the farmworkers what the King Ranch people have, we would be making some real progress."

Perhaps the most prominent Kineño was Lauro Cavazos, who came to the ranch in 1912 and served as foreman of the Santa Gertrudis division for forty-three years. All five of his children earned college degrees. Three of his sons graduated from Texas Tech University and made their mark in the outside world. In 1980 Dr. Lauro ("Larry") Cavazos became president of Texas Tech and its medical school. In August 1988, President Ronald Reagan nominated him as secretary of education. After being confirmed by the U.S. Senate, Dr. Cavazos became the first Hispanic to serve in the Cabinet. One of his brothers, Richard, is a retired four-star army general, served as commander of Fort Hood, and earned two Distinguished Service Crosses. Another brother, Bobby Cavazos, was an All-America running back at Texas Tech before going into the ranching business.

had earlier paid $400 for "one large closed carriage and harness" at Corpus Christi to carry the couple on their honeymoon to the Santa Gertrudis, or "King's Folly," as the bride's friends called it. The newlyweds were escorted by armed *vaqueros* on the four-day trip. "Captain King" and Etta (or Pet), their names for each other, happily settled into their first home, an adobe hut so small that she had to hang her pots and pans outside. Etta added her Bible and polish to this rough, dangerous environment and was a model of propriety in demanding civilized behavior in her home. She proved to be an excellent helpmate, hostess, and guardian of the health and welfare of her Kineños.

In his memoirs, Rip Ford called King's moving his family from Brownsville to the cow camp "an undertaking of great danger" and "an act of extreme audacity." Ford had high praise for their new home, describing it as follows:

> The camp of Capt. King had been the seat of hospitality. In it all found welcome. Much was due to the lady-like management of Mrs. King. The guest was reminded of the baronial halls of England which in days gone by were open to all well-behaved comers. On the part of the Texas rancher there was no attempt at display. The viands were easy of reach and abundant. There was a republican simplicity reigning supreme which made all feel comfortable and at home. All were treated as equals whose bearing gave guarantees of respectability . . .
>
> His daughter (Henrietta King) was noted for her culture, her capacity, and her beauty. She was the wise counsellor of her husband, his faithful confidant in whom he placed implicit trust . . . Yet her demeanor was free from objection. She was meek in deportment, . . .
>
> Santa Gertrudis was deemed a charmed spot on the sea of danger — once within its walls all risks vanished for the time being. The wayfarer felt he was in a circle that violence could not enter.

Captain King lost a close friend and trusted partner on April 14, 1855, when Legs Lewis was shot to death by an irate husband at Corpus Christi. Lewis was in the midst of a campaign for Congress when Dr. J. T. Yarrington killed him with a blast from a double-barreled shotgun. The doctor discovered that his wife and Legs were having an affair when he intercepted some of their love letters. After the couple separated, Yarrington was paid three visits by Lewis, who demanded all the letters so they could not be used against him politically. After failing to get the correspondence, the unarmed Legs was killed the fourth time he badgered the wronged doctor at his office.

Bachelor Lewis died without heirs or a will, so his estate was settled by administrators appointed by the Probate Court of Nueces County. Since the deceased owned undivided half-interest in two of his grants, Captain King had a partner, Maj. W. W. Chapman, present when the Lewis property was offered at public sale in Corpus Christi on July 1, 1856. Chapman offered the winning bid of $1,575 for the Rincon grant but was abruptly transferred to California, leaving the hard-pressed King alone to make a late full payment on the note.

In late December 1856, Richard persuaded another friend, Capt. James Walworth, a steamboater and investor, to pay $5,000 for the larger de la Garza Santa Gertrudis grant. Although Walworth kept title to the land and paid taxes on it, King had actual control since he owned the livestock and equipment on the property.

After a lengthy stay on the Santa Gertrudis, the Kings moved back to Brownsville to a cottage on Elizabeth Street next to the Kenedys. They were among the affluent Brick House Crowd, but Etta preferred homemaking and church activities to the frivolity of town society. The Kings divided their time between the two households before establishing their legal residence at the ranch in December 1860. Their first child, Henrietta Marie ("Nettie") was born in their town cottage on April

17, 1856. A second daughter, Ella Morse, arrived on April 13, 1858.

Rains and army contracts brought a surge of steamboat business to the firm of M. Kenedy & Co. in 1856. A Kenedy trip to Washington, D.C., resulted in a contract to transport U.S. Army supplies on the Rio Grande, and in November, the company presented bills for services totaling more than $17,000 to the quartermaster at Fort Brown.

During a trip upriver in the fall of 1856, Captain King struck up a warm friendship with Lt. Col. Robert E. Lee, who was sitting on a court-martial in session at Ringgold Barracks. Richard was much impressed by the bearing and character of the older Lee, who later had supper at the King home and attended church services with them while sitting on another court-martial at Fort Brown. During the long adjournments of the court, Richard and Robert hunted on horseback together and visited the Santa Gertrudis, where engineer Lee was asked to recommend a building site for a permanent ranch house. He chose the highest point on the prairie, a little rise on the banks of Santa Gertrudis Creek. King held Lee in high esteem and never forgot his advice to "buy land — and never sell."

After being appointed commander of the Department of Texas in March 1860, Colonel Lee was ordered to stop border raids by Juan Cortina along the lower Rio Grande. During this campaign his friend King kept his troops supplied with a special wagon train. Once the Cortina raids into Texas stopped in May 1860, Lee spent the night at the new Santa Gertrudis ranch house en route to his San Antonio headquarters.[3]

---

[3] In 1867 the Kings made a trip to Kentucky, where the captain purchased some blooded stallions. The family then traveled to Virginia just to visit with an old friend, Robert E. Lee, who was then the president of Washington College at Lexington. After seeing his four-year-old King namesake for the first time, the famed Confederate leader wryly remarked that he liked the little boy's fine new suit except for the color — it was blue! During this visit, Captain King re-

Sometime in 1858, the Kings moved from their adobe *jacal* to the "original" ranch house, the site of the present great *hacienda* built by Robert Kleberg in 1912. This new home was a low, rambling frame building with a half second story and bannistered front gallery. It was connected by an unroofed walkway with a detached stone kitchen and dining room, as well as eating and sleeping quarters for extra hands. To the north was a watchtower and a stone commissary. Nearby was a line of small houses for the Kineños and their families. A one-room school for the ranch children was started in the 1860s.

In those early days before the mesquite invaded the treeless prairie, the site chosen for rounding up half-wild Longhorns was the cooling shade of a motte of anaqua trees along the Tranquitas dam and tank, where the Kleberg County Courthouse is now located. Mrs. King and the children would bring a wagon there at noon, spread a bountiful lunch on a shaded blanket, and eat with the captain.

The earliest cattle brand was designed by Richard and called the "Ere Flecha" ꓤ . After marrying Etta, he used another brand made from her initials, an H and K connected ﴾ . This was the first King Ranch brand officially recorded in the brand registry of Nueces County on March 20, 1859. On June 27 of that year, he registered the "Ere Flecha" along with two other brands, an L and K connected ꓘ for the Lewis and King partnership and "King and Walworth's Brand," which added a V at the top of the L and K ꓦ . For the first several years, all livestock at the Santa Gertrudis carried one of these four brands.

The ranch's first receipts came from sales of horses and mules for U.S. Army wagon trains. By the late 1850s, Captain King was also selling fleshy, strong cattle as breed stock to Monterrey and Saltillo ranchers, who paid from $12 to $18 a head. He was also shipping cattle by steamer to New Orleans, while the proximity of

---

ceived an autographed new photograph of General Lee, which is proudly preserved today in the King Ranch vault.

Corpus Christi made it his supply point. His ultimate goal was to ship meat rather than resort to long trail drives; to that end, he tried to preserve beef carcasses by infusing a strong brine injection into the veins of freshly slaughtered cattle. When the experiment failed, his Kineños poured the tallow into barrels, hung the hides on fences, and cast the meat to some 7,000 hogs.

The King family was out of Texas during the fall of 1859, most likely to accompany Etta's half-brother, Hiram Chamberlain, when he enrolled at Centre College in Danville, Kentucky. During the trip the captain purchased some horses for shipment to Texas. By June 1860, he was back at Brownsville, angrily filing claims against the United States government for damages suffered during the Cortina raids. The uprising had idled all the steamboats of M. Kenedy & Co., and King was asking for $250,000 to cover company losses. Although Washington refused to consider these damage claims, Richard did make a pointed protest against the federal government's inability to protect its own border. Even as talk of secession and Civil War increased in 1860, Mifflin Kenedy was in Pittsburgh ordering another big boat and two upriver mudskimmers; if war did come, the company would have seven steamboats to handle a potential trade boom.

It was a Cortina raid on his San Salvador del Tule grant that convinced Kenedy that his ranch pastures were too close to the volatile Rio Grande. Thus he prudently decided to drive all of his 1,595 cattle and 87 horses to the relative safety of the Santa Gertrudis and become a ranching partner of his oldest and best friend. On December 5, 1860, the new firm of R. King & Co. was organized to include the King livestock, ranch improvements, and land titles to Rincon, the Agua Dulce, and one-half of the de la Garza Santa Gertrudis. The shares were divided three ways: three-eighths to King, three-eighths to Kenedy, and two-eighths to James Walworth. By 1861, R. King & Co. owned 20,000 head of cattle and 3,000 horses. It was during this period that the captain moved his family from Brownsville back to the ranch for good, prompting Richard King II to later joke that he was "born in a stagecoach while mother was hurrying to Brownsville" on December 15, 1860. A fourth King child, Alice Gertrudis, was born on April 29, 1862.

Both Richard and Mifflin were staunch Democrats and States' Rights men, so when Texas voted to secede from the Union, they were recognized as Confederates during the Civil War. The conflict proved to be a bonanza for the opportunistic partners, who got rich selling supplies to the Confederacy in exchange for gold. During the war, Texas was divided into three areas, with Col. Rip Ford named commander of the Military Department of the Rio Grande. His charge was to protect the river trade and cultivate friendly relations with neutral Mexico. When Ford and 1,500 Texas troops arrived at Brazos Santiago in February 1861, he found King and Kenedy ready with steamboats and willing to shuttle Confederate troops.

After the Union naval blockade was extended to include the Texas coast in July 1861, Captain Kenedy stayed at Brownsville to manage the boats. King, on the other hand, was already furnishing contract beef and salt to Confederate forces. His Santa Gertrudis ranch was soon to be a major depot for Confederate cotton sent to Europe by way of the neutral Mexican port of Bagdad.

By late 1861, the Union naval blockade left the South with a baled cotton crop waiting to be sold and desperately needed by England's huge textile industry. South of the Rio Grande and off its mouth were the open waters of Bagdad, where Southern cotton could be delivered to neutral European cargo ships anchored offshore, thus evading the American blockade. This Confederacy "back door" created an immediate cotton boom since the trade was for hard money at Matamoros. The cotton road came across the pastures of King and Kenedy to the decks of their steamboats, which delivered the cotton to neutral ships offshore. In March 1862, Richard's Santa

Gertrudis ranch headquarters was designated as the official Confederate receiving, storage, and shipping point for cotton bales from East Texas, Louisiana, Arkansas, and Missouri. That spring, Kenedy & Co. steamers first resorted to the ruse of Mexican ownership and registry; even though they flew the Mexican flag, there was no change in crew, and Kenedy continued to supervise the operation from an office in Matamoros. Mexican cotton speculators were even buying their cotton *in* Texas before it crossed the river and paying in gold. Even more cotton was funneled across King's pasture road after Union forces captured New Orleans in April 1862; it was common to see twenty-mule team wagons hauling twelve bales each toward the Rio Grande.

By October 1862, Bagdad and the mouth of the Rio Grande had achieved status as a world port — the only Confederate entry point where foreign munitions and medical supplies could be exchanged for cotton. The enormous impact of this "back door" is revealed in the following figures: Cotton prices in East Texas went from 10 cents a pound in 1861 to 82 cents a pound in 1864; the number of ships anchored off Bagdad beach jumped from twenty in September 1862 to as many as 300 by early 1865.

Richard King had taken on the title and duties of quartermaster's agent and was absent when a British military observer named Fremantle paid a short visit to the Santa Gertrudis in April 1863. Upon leaving, the impressed foreigner noted:

> We now entered upon a boundless and most fertile prairie, upon which, as far as the eye could reach, cattle were feeding. Bulls and cows, horses and mares . . . all seemed sleek and in good condition, yet they get nothing but what they can pick up on the prairie.

On April 28, 1863, M. Kenedy & Co. contracted to supply all of the Confederate forces stationed on the border, the Rio Grande sub-district of the Trans-Mississippi Department. The Confederate government paid for the supplies with delivered cotton; on a cost-plus percentage, this contract brought about $60,000 in gold for each of the three partners.

On November 1, 1863, an invasion of the lower Texas coast involving twenty-six Union transports and 7,000 troops began with the occupation of Brazos Santiago. Two days later, panic-stricken Confederate General Hamilton Bee torched Fort Brown, burned the cotton yard, and abandoned Brownsville. Many townspeople found refuge across the river in Matamoros while stores and homes were looted after dark. When a cache of gunpowder caught fire and exploded, a fire was triggered that destroyed two city blocks, including the riverfront offices of M. Kenedy & Co. General Bee led a small wagon train in a hasty retreat north and compounded the crisis by destroying every cotton wagon train he met. On November 6, Maj. Gen. Nathaniel Banks occupied Brownsville with no resistance offered, then left Maj. Gen. N. J. T. Dana in charge of all Union troops on the Rio Grande. Captain King's old foe, Juan Cortina, the acting governor of Tamaulipas, ended the cotton-shipping charade by turning three of Richard's boats — the *Matamoros*, the *Mustang,* and the *James Hale* — over to Dana, who used them to haul Union troops and supplies.

During the Union occupation of Brownsville, King and his family, including the old and ailing Reverend Chamberlain, were at the Santa Gertrudis. Bagdad was still open to neutral shipping, and the captain kept the cotton moving by diverting cotton trains west to upriver crossings at Laredo and Eagle Pass, then into Mexico. General Dana responded by hiring thugs and killers to wreak havoc on the new cotton roads while his spies kept an eye on "rebel agent" King and his ranch.

On December 22, 1863, a friend told Richard that Union Captain James Speed and a force of sixty cavalrymen would attempt to capture him that night. The ranch foreman, Capt. James Richardson, had organized 150 employees in a well-armed Confederate home guard, but they were away at the time. Since Henrietta was seven months pregnant, her husband decided to go underground alone, gambling that his family would not be harmed if he was absent, and no resistance was offered to a search. King left a senior ranch hand, Francisco Alvarado, in charge of the family and instructed him to sleep in the ranch house that night.

Keeping vigil on a cot in the hall, Alvarado was awakened by rifle fire toward daybreak, rushed out on the front porch unarmed, and shouted, "Don't fire on this house! There is a family here —" Those were Francisco's last words as he fell dead from a single ball. The Union raiders carried his body into the parlor, lit a lamp, and discovered that the corpse was not their intended target, Richard King. After searching, looting, and wrecking the place, Speed's men occupied ranch headquarters until Christmas Eve before fleeing from Richardson's returning company. On Christmas morning Etta, her father, and the children took a coach north to San Patricio, where Robert E. Lee King was born on February 22, 1864. The fatherless family soon moved to the safety of San Antonio. Richard spent eighteen months keeping the cotton trains moving, delivering beef and supplies to Confederate troops, and serving as a private in Captain Richardson's company.

While King's ranch was abandoned, weeks of bitter cold and ice during the winter of 1863–64 caused "The Big Drift" as huge herds of cattle from Central and North Texas put the freezing northers to their backs and drifted south to the warmth and grass of the gulf shores. Many would remain unclaimed on the Santa Gertrudis after the war.

On December 22, 1863, General John Magruder ordered Rip Ford to raise the Cavalry of the West at San Antonio and clean out Union forces on the Rio Grande. With help from Maj. Santos Benavides and his Thirty-third Texas Cavalry, Ford forced the new Union commander, Maj. Gen. Francis J. Herron, to withdraw from all upriver outposts by June 1864, leaving only Brownsville and the port of Brazos Santiago under Yankee occupation. The fever-ridden Rip and his "Expeditionary Forces" of 1,200 volunteers recaptured Brownsville unopposed on July 30, 1864, enabling Confederate cotton to be re-routed there directly through King's ranch. By the end of the year, Mexican "owners" had regained possession of all the M. Kenedy & Co. steamboats. In the final months of the Civil War, Richard King recouped his losses and made large profits in gold by trading cotton, supplying Confederate troops, and running steamers and wagon trains.

After General Lee surrendered on April 9, 1865, Union troops occupied Brownsville on May 30 while Captain King found refuge in Matamoros. By terms of the Amnesty Proclamation, he had to apply for a presidential pardon since he owned taxable property valued at more than $20,000. Richard's friend Rip Ford was serving as commissioner of paroles for area Confederate troops and helped him draft a formal request for amnesty. On September 15, 1865, King wrote a letter to Maj. Gen. Giles S. Smith, the commander at Brownsville, asking for the return of his house on Elizabeth Street so he could be reunited with his family coming from San Antonio. The request read in part:

> It is my intention to resume my residence in Brownsville, as a citizen of the United States, obedient to the law of the land and to the constituted authorities. I say this candidly and frankly, and I am persuaded that you will believe me.

After his request was granted, the grateful rancher took the opportunity to repay Ford for his timely assistance. The rigors of the war left Rip broken in health and too sickly to work for two years. The desperate ex-Confederate, who had a wife and eight children to support, was rescued by Captain King, who anonymously paid his house rent and deposited $250 a month in Ford's bank account during his period of disability.

Richard spent eighteen months in Brownsville putting the steamboat business back in order and reorganizing after losing two partners. Charles Stillman had withdrawn from the firm of M. Kenedy & Co. before the spring of 1865, with James Walworth taking over his interest. Shortly after James's death in April 1865, King and Kenedy paid his widow Jane $50,000 in cash for her husband's interest in both M. Kenedy & Co. and R. King & Co. Richard and Mifflin retrieved the three old steamers seized by Union forces, but constant service soon wore them out. In the meantime, the partners ordered four expensive and specially designed new boats from Pittsburgh: the *Antonio, Eugenia, Tamaulipas* and *Camargo*. All were operating on the Rio Grande by late summer of 1865. Early the next year, the *Enterprise* and *El Primero* were added to the steamer fleet to stifle competition. Once both partners were pardoned, they resumed their old business of hauling freight for the U.S. Army, and the boat company was reorganized as the firm of King, Kenedy & Co. in the summer of 1866. The new business had a capital stock of $250,000; both men owned twenty-five percent interest in the company, and Kenedy served as active manager. During this period their former associate, the ailing Charles Stillman, left Brownsville for good and spent his last years at Cornwall-on-the-Hudson in New York, where his money started the National City Bank of New York.

On October 1, 1866, King, Kenedy & Co. received a charter from the state legislature for the exclusive rights to build a railway from Brazos Santiago or Point Isabel to Brownsville. Evidently, they were simply trying to ward off rail competition, for they did nothing except buy a few right-of-way tracts for this phantom line. Some angry Brownsville merchants, resentful of their high steamer freight rates, persuaded the legislature to revoke the charter in 1870, and saw that it was granted to a group of "anti-monopolists" who organized the Rio Grande Railroad Company. By 1871, twenty-two and a half miles of track were operational, from Point Isabel to Brownsville, in spite of two unsuccessful obstructive lawsuits brought by King and Kenedy.

Mother Nature also threw her full fury against the partners. A hurricane that struck in September 1867 sank four of their steamers and destroyed their facilities at Brazos Santiago and Bagdad. Richard viewed this damage as a sign to leave the river for good and move his family back to the Santa Gertrudis. Mifflin also turned his full attention to ranching in the fall of 1868, leaving his son-in-law Dalzell in charge of an ever-diminishing steamer business. In May 1874, the two partners sold out and Capt. William Kelly took over the company. Eventually, only one small steamer, the *Bessie,* was left to earn a livelihood for Kelly before it, too, ceased operations in 1903.

By 1866, the assets of R. King & Co. included undivided half-interests in parcels of land totaling more than 146,000 acres. The partners estimated they owned 84,000 cattle and 5,400 horses. In November 1867, Richard and Mifflin decided to separate their shares in the ranch and equally divide their herds. In June 1868, Kenedy signed papers to purchase the neighboring twenty-six leagues of the Laureles grant from Charles Stillman. By February 1870, Mifflin had dissolved his partnership with Richard and had completed payment on the last of three equal notes for his independent ranch, the Laureles. Building post-and-plank fences around their separate ranches was the first step with this project, beginning in 1868. By December, Kenedy had completed a thirty-mile line of fence from the Oso to the Laureles Creek, enclosing 131,000 acres of his new purchase. This was the first fenced range west of the Mississippi and was bounded on two sides by Laguna Madre. Richard King had a greater task enclosing his inland pastures, but he managed to fence the Santa Gertrudis by the close of the decade, using 1x6x20 planks made of Louisiana cypress and pine as fencing material.

One task remained for the ex-partners: the dividing

of their joint herd. In January 1869, King and Kenedy hired 100 *vaqueros* to round up their cattle. When the count was completed that November, 25,000 head of cattle were branded at the Rancho de Los Laureles, while King branded 23,664 head at Rancho Santa Gertrudis. He was also allowed to keep the estimated 10,000 head ungathered "on the prairie." Thus the roundup showed that R. King & Co. owned 58,664 head of cattle, along with 4,400 horses.

It should be noted that the partners owned 84,000 head at the close of the Civil War. During normal seasons, cattle increase at the rate of one-third a year, thus doubling the original stock every three years. Taking into account the 1,000 cattle they sold during this period, the two should have counted a total of 167,000 head, not the 58,664 head they found. The missing 108,336 cattle had been stolen by Mexican cattle raiders and taken across the Rio Grande.

On February 26, 1870, an Agreement and Final Settlement was signed concluding the affairs of R. King & Co. With the partnership officially dissolved, Richard King was now the sole owner of the Santa Gertrudis and needed a new brand, the famous Running W ƲƲ that was registered in Nueces County on February 9, 1869. Legend has it that the brand represents either the Santa Gertrudis Creek or a moving rattlesnake. In Spanish, it is named the Viborita, the Little Snake. Captain King chose the Running W for several reasons: Rustlers would find it hard to alter by later burning; it was open-spaced with no crossing of lines, thus leaving no deep spots that invite screw worms; it was a good-looking brand.

Richard's next goal was to purchase the 350,000 acres making up the San Juan de Carricitos grant, a huge tract with an old water hole and *rancho* called El Sauz that was sixty miles south of the Santa Gertrudis. He was deeded his first interest in this land in September 1873, but the total purchase was not completed until May 1889.

The decade of the 1870s was to be the stormiest and

most profitable period in Captain King's life. At the same time King cattle were being trailed north to the Kansas railheads, he was fighting a bitter rear-guard battle to protect his property and life from Mexican cattle thieves. After the Texas Rangers were disbanded by the Reconstruction regime, South Texas cowmen had only the indifferent protection offered by garrisons of U.S. troops; in effect, they were left to shift for themselves against Mexican raiders, who cynically boasted that "the *gringos* are raising cows for me." While King was building fence, ranch foreman Richardson was patrolling the area. Preventing theft was a major reason for fencing the ranch. The captain hired agents on the Rio Grande to try to return his branded stock, purchased thirty stands of Henry rifles and ammunition for his *vaqueros,* and employed a dozen extra riders. He always traveled with a shotgun and four armed Kineños.

On the road from the ranch to Brownsville, King positioned stage camps stocked with fast horses at twenty-mile intervals. Such speed in relays was critical; as he later said, "I had to travel fast. My life depended on it." Because of such precautions, he was never robbed or successfully ambushed, although he often carried as much as $50,000 in a steel box hidden inside his road coach.

After the Civil War, Juan Cortina held the rank of brigadier general and commander of the Line of the Bravo in the Mexican army. It was Cortina who organized the cattle raids into Texas and protected the Mexican raiders. He stocked four ranches in Tamaulipas with cows and horses stolen in Texas; in fact, a Brownsville grand jury in 1872 called Cortina the "ranking cow and horse thief on both frontiers." In peak years between 1865 and 1878, as many as 200,000 Texas cattle were stolen by Mexican raiders, who often resorted to brutal murder and sometimes skinned cattle alive. Juan's special target was an old enemy he swore to capture and hang, Richard King.

In a concerted effort to stop wholesale cattle theft, cowmen organized the Stock Raisers Association of Western Texas in 1870. Mifflin Kenedy presided over the first meeting. Their first move was an agreement to advertise their brands in local papers. In May 1872, the Grant administration sent three commissioners to investigate alleged disorders along the Rio Grande. The commission took sworn testimony from hundreds of eyewitnesses from July 30 to October 3; in a strong report submitted to Congress, they documented in detail the cattle losses to Mexican raiders. Nothing was done. When witness King appeared before the commission on August 26, 1872, he asserted that there was no security whatever for life or property on the frontier. To prove his point, he told of giving a ride to a stranger, Franz Specht, while traveling to Brownsville to testify. After dark, King's coach was ambushed by Mexican assassins; Specht was killed by their gunfire.

By 1875, many fearful owners simply deserted their ranches in the Wild Horse Desert, but not King and Kenedy, who were determined to defend themselves and their families. In March of that year, King's ranch was besieged by a large party of Mexican bandits; border legend has it that the raiders attacked but were given a sound beating before melting away.

Captain King soon had a formidable ally to join the fray. In late 1874, newly elected Democratic Governor Richard Coke reestablished the Texas Rangers. The following April, Capt. L. H. McNelly was commissioned to enlist a Ranger company for special duty on the lower Rio Grande. With only forty-one men, this small, frail, soft-spoken tubercular managed to tame the Nueces Strip in less than a year. In carrying out his own private war on Mexican cattle thieves, the fearless McNelly followed a brutal policy of terror, made law as he went, took no prisoners, and illegally invaded Mexico even as he defied the U.S. army and government. The Stock Raisers Association provided his war chest while Captain King supplied McNelly's men with beef and good horses, and twice sent cash bonuses for their work.

Lee McNelly's most spectacular feat was a raid across the Rio Grande, in November 1875, to recover stolen Texas cattle from the Las Cuevas ranch of Gen. Juan Flores, the chief of the border cow thieves. As a result of this daring strike into Mexico, Lee forced the Mexicans to return seventy-five head of stolen cattle at Camargo. On November 22, four young McNelly rangers, including George Durham, were ordered to take the thirty-five stolen cows carrying Richard King's "Running W" brand to his Santa Gertrudis ranch.[4] The captain was amazed at McNelly's feat and remarked:

> That was a daring trip. There is not another man in the world who could invade a foreign country with that number of men and all get back alive. Captain McNelly is the first man that ever got stolen cattle out of Mexico. Out of thousands of head I have had stolen, these are the only ones I ever got back, and I think more of them than of any five hundred head I have.

The famed rancher ordered his hands to saw off the right horn of each cow, then turned them out on the big range to graze in peace for life.

Border cattle raids dropped dramatically as news of McNelly's strike spread through northern Mexico. A near-end to border depredations came after Porfirio Díaz assumed power in 1877. American supporters in Brownsville had loaned him funds in early 1876 in return for Díaz's promise to remove Cortina from his post on the border. The new Mexican president named a new commander for the Line of the Bravo, then sent for Cortina, and held him under house arrest in Mexico City until his death.

---

[4] After Texas governor Richard B. Hubbard disbanded McNelly's Special Force, George Durham returned to the Santa Gertrudis in 1878, and Captain King hired him to do ranch police work. In 1882 George married King's niece, Caroline Chamberlain, and was named general foreman of the El Sauz rancho, a position he held until his death in 1940. As of 1986, Durham's grandson, Lavoyger, was the third-generation foreman of what had become the Norias Division of the King Ranch.

After the Civil War, there were huge herds of untended Texas cattle on the South Texas prairies. Three-year-old steers worth $5 in Texas would bring $20 in gold from a northern buyer at Abilene, Kansas. With such an economic incentive, Texas Longhorn herds were on the long trail to the Kansas railheads by early summer of 1866; five years later, 700,000 Texas cattle were trailed north. It is interesting to note that the words "trail" and "driver" do not appear in the Santa Gertrudis account books; Captain King put his cattle on the "road," and they were driven by "Kansas men." Between November 1869 and August 1872, he sold 13,500 head. By the end of the decade, Richard had sent over 100,000 cattle north and made a profit of well over one million dollars.

King kept in touch with his trail drivers by letter and telegram, then traveled to meet the herds and personally sell them to northern buyers. He also hired James H. Stevens as his livestock broker and agent for the Kansas, St. Louis, Kansas City, and Chicago markets. His Longhorns were gathered in late February or early March, then moved north with the advancing spring grass at a pace of ten to twelve miles a day for 100 days. Their destination was Abilene, Kansas, until 1875; then the herds were sold at Dodge City. King ranch herds ran from one to four thousand head on the trail, and they often moved in separate sections. His crews typically consisted of a trail boss, ten drovers, a cook, and a wrangler for the remuda of extra mounts. They were on the "road" from early spring to late summer, then back on the home range by fall.

Unlike other cowmen, Richard did not hire his trail bosses for the normal $100 a month in wages; instead, his herd bosses were ranch foremen and profit-sharing partners. They signed contracts making them actual owners of the herd and road outfit and actual employers of all hands. After they purchased the herd at the current Texas price, Captain King paid all expenses. The two evenly split the net profits, the difference after road expenses between the price of the herd at the Santa Gertrudis and the price the boss got in Kansas. A good boss who could avoid trail losses thus had the opportunity to make a much higher profit than ordinary wages. One such example was boss John Fitch, the foreman at Agua Dulce. On March 12, 1875, Fitch contracted with King to buy 4,737 head of beef cattle at $12 a head. They were trailed in four separate herds and sold at Denison, Texas, on July 21 at an average of $18.44 per head. On this one abbreviated drive, Richard made a $50,000 net profit, a performance he repeated scores of times in the boom years of the 1870s.

Since the rawboned, sinewy Longhorns did not produce choice grades of beef, a major goal of Captain King was to improve the quality of his herds. To this end, he imported 100 Durhams, mostly bulls, from Kentucky in late 1872. After the "Black Friday" panic on Wall Street on September 19, 1873, tighter credit and a plunge in beef prices ensued. Richard had already sold his 1873 herd and rode out the financial storm by concentrating on his hide and tallow works, selling horses and mules, and marketing wool from his sheep flocks during 1874.

On February 7, 1874, an awed reporter from the *Corpus Christi Gazette* recorded his impressions of King's ranch:

> The main rancho, Santa Gertrudis, is situated on a high hill between the Santa Gertrudis and San Fernando creeks. A tower or lookout, erected on the top of a large brick warehouse, commands an extended view, the eye taking in at one glance a scope of country for twenty miles around. The sight is delightful, combining the pleasant with the picturesque. On this hill the Captain has erected a large and commodious dwelling with the necessary out-houses . . . The houses for his vaqueros are constructed with a view to comfort and durability, at a respectful distance from the main house. A neat and substantial picket fence encloses several acres of Bermuda grass; its appearance in

118

Spring resembling a well cultivated park, interspersed
here and there with beautiful shade trees . . .

The reporter noted that this "mammoth rancho" of 78,225
acres included forty miles of fencing and had a work force
of over 100 men. The stock of the *rancho* included 50,000
head of cattle, 6,000 horses and mules, a flock of 30,000
Merino sheep, and 7,000 hogs. Marveling at the self-con-
tained nature of the ranch operation, he commented: "The
work prosecuted under his [King's] supervision and from
the forging of a horseshoe nail to the erection of a first class
house, can all be accomplished by those living upon the
rancho." In addition to this tract, the reporter wrote that
Captain King owned the Rincon de Santa Gertrudis
(15,500 acres), the Agua Dulce (33,631 acres), 13,284 acres
of Padre Island, 15,000 acres on the Saus Creek, two
leagues at San Diego, and the twenty-five leagues known
as the San Juan de Carricitos.

Ranch headquarters was home to the five King children: Nettie, Ella, Alice, Richard, and Lee. By 1867 the
frame house was remodeled, with an addition to the main
living quarters and a second story added to provide bed-
rooms for the children. Mrs. McGuire, a governess from
Virginia, and Professor Allen, a tutor, helped Henrietta
with the girls and boys. After Reverend Chamberlain
died at Brownsville in November 1866, Etta's half brothers — Hiram, Jr., Bland, Willie, and Edwin — moved to
the ranch. Of the four, only Bland spent his life as a
ranch employee.

The tenderhearted Captain King was a very indul-
gent husband and father who openly spoiled his "pets."
When he gave his wife some showy diamond earrings,
Mrs. King had the jeweler cover them with dark enamel
to avoid the appearance of display. In 1870, fifteen-year-
old Nettie enrolled at Henderson Female Institute, a
Presbyterian girls school at Danville, Kentucky. She was
later joined there by her two younger sisters, but the
three King girls were back on the ranch by the fall of

1875. Ella and Alice were back in school the next year, this time at Mrs. Cuthbert's Seminary at St. Louis. When their father was in the city on cattle business, he stayed at the Southern Hotel and always had diamond gifts in hand when he visited his daughters.

When he was fifteen, Richard King II enrolled at Centre Presbyterian College at Danville. It was said that this handsome lad made heads turn whenever he traveled about town with his own carriage and manservant. After young Richard graduated in 1878, younger brother Lee started college there the next year but did not finish. Lee, the quieter and more serious of the two, chose instead to transfer to a business college at St. Louis, thinking that a knowledge of accounting would be helpful on the ranch. Of the five King children, the two youngest, Lee and Alice, loved ranch life the most.

It seems that the King girls were often ashamed of their famous father's rough, unkempt appearance. In some of the family portraits, the rest of the clan look freshly scrubbed and dressed while the old captain appears to have stopped ranch work just long enough to pose. Indeed, he made a striking figure with his wide-brimmed black hat, black string tie, dark broadcloth coat, rumpled pants, and always-scuffed boots. His black beard reached the second button of his shirt. King had a slight limp, most likely caused when his leg was broken by a moving anchor chain on a steamboat. In fact, his *vaqueros* referred to the boss as El Cojo, the Lame One. The captain also had a noticeably disfigured left nostril; it seems that when he gifted Etta with a parrot, the bird bit him on the nose and the wound never healed properly.

Always a rough-and-tumble frontiersman, Richard liked nothing better than a good bare-knuckle fistfight while snorting his "Rose Bud Whiskey." Legend has it that he hired a tough Irishman whose main job was to take on the boss when the captain was in the mood. J. Frank Dobie once heard the following story from an old drover named Branch Isbell:

King was a rough old devil. One time a man named

Kelley who was working for him said, "Captain King, if you were not such a rich man and a captain, you wouldn't cuss me as you do.' 'Damn you,' King replied, jerking off his hat, 'forget the riches and the captain title and let's fight.' The two fought for half an hour in a slaughterhouse where they mingled their blood with that of the cattle. Then they shook hands in mutual admiration.

He spent his adult life commanding others and barking out orders in a brusque manner, and even his closest friend, Mifflin Kenedy, admitted that King was "violently opinionated." This same ogre, however, was a soft touch for hardluck stories, would drop everything to spring a Kineño from jail or help a friend, and was known to tiptoe in sock feet to bring cold lemonade to a ranch visitor's room.

When he died, Captain King was the greatest cattle baron in Texas, owning ranch property totaling 614,000 acres. A point should be made about his gigantic pastures: Richard was careful to observe legality in acquiring more than sixty tracts of land, in addition to the two original purchases. Working through his Brownsville lawyers, first Stephen Powers and then Jim Wells, the captain *bought* every piece of land he owned. These two formidable attorneys kept their client out of the courts and free from litigation for more than thirty years. Many of King's purchases involved jigsaw puzzles of Spanish and Mexican land grants, often with indefinite and overlapping boundaries. Powers and Wells had to deal with multiple heirs of the original grantee and buy up their undivided interest. Working through their law offices and the courts, the two lawyers doggedly pursued title to a piece of land until King had it.

Two examples point to the difficulties they encountered. Although Richard's first land purchase, the Rincon de Santa Gertrudis, came in 1853, the title fight took thirty years before he was the uncontested owner of the land. In the other example, Jim Wells was initially hired simply to buy legitimate claims to undivided interests and to clear title to King Ranch lands, a task that took seven years.

After Stephen Powers's partner was killed in a duel in the spring of 1878, the vacancy was filled four months later by twenty-eight-year-old James B. "Jim" Wells, a graduate of the University of Virginia law school. The friendly, outgoing Wells was fluent in Spanish, and the old captain took a liking to him, putting Jim on retainer to buy *derechos* (rights) for land King wanted. When Powers died in February 1882, Richard was deeply moved by the loss of his "old and true friend." In a letter to the junior partner, he lamented, "There is not a man in this State, less yourself, misses him more than myself. God bless him and his dear family." After choosing Wells to continue as his attorney, the captain advanced him money to buy law books along with these instructions: "Young man, the only thing I want to hear from you is when I can move my fences."

In the 1870s Richard branched out in several new business directions. He became a director of the Corpus Christi Navigation Company in 1871. The company had been formed to dredge a channel deep and wide enough to make the city a major port. Within three years, the channel was deep enough to handle scheduled calls by Morgan Line Steamers. In 1877, King and Kenedy purchased interest in the *Corpus Christi Free Press,* forerunner of the *Caller-Times.* The next year Captain King built the first ice plant in Brownsville, with the objective of refrigerating his beef products. Simply to improve the service, he purchased a stage line and contracted with the federal government to carry mail and passengers on two routes, San Antonio to Brownsville and Corpus Christi to Laredo. After buying five stagecoaches and putting son Richard in charge, the Kings owned the service for a decade. However, they never showed a profit due to one sticky problem: too many friends rode on passes. Once he was made aware of the situation, the old captain decreed the new policy that *nobody* would ride free. When some of his old cronies complained, however, he gave in and remarked, "Guess we'll have to waive the new order this time."

In March 1875, the Texas legislature chartered the Corpus Christi, San Diego & Rio Grande Narrow Gauge Railroad to connect Corpus Christi and Laredo by rail. Among the chief financial backers were King and Kenedy, while Richard actually purchased a locomotive for the enterprise. When the company was sold to the Mexican National Railway, its name was changed to the Texas Mexican Railway, and the rail line was completed to Laredo in November 1881. To celebrate this historic occasion, a special train, the "King and Kenedy Excursion," made the inaugural trip. The two longtime friends dispensed hospitality to a hundred of the original backers from their private car, the "Malinche," hitched to the end of the train. En route, Captain King served his favorite Rose Bud whiskey and spiked the lemonade bowl with champagne. By the time they reached their destination, the whole party of South Texas dignitaries was roaring drunk and ended up parading through Laredo behind a big bass drum, singing at the top of their lungs and challenging all comers to a fight.

By the early 1880s, this "Tex-Mex" railroad was carrying a train of twenty-eight cattle cars, and Collins Station on the line was only twenty miles from the Santa Gertrudis headquarters. For many years Collins Station, five miles east of present-day Alice, was the mailing address for "King's Rancho."

When Alice King graduated as class salutatorian from Mrs. Cuthbert's Seminary at St. Louis in 1881, Richard II was courting her classmate and best friend, Pearl Ashbrook. By then, Alice's two older sisters had married and were living in the city. In November 1878, Nettie King married Maj. E. B. Atwood, U.S. Army Quartermaster Department, against her father's wishes. The captain was present at the wedding ceremony in the Lindell Hotel, however, and a St. Louis newspaper reported that the bride received more than $10,000 worth of wedding gifts. In 1881, Ella King married Louis M. Welton, a merchant with business interests in St. Louis and San Antonio, with the ceremony taking place at the Santa Gertrudis ranch house.

Mrs. King was soon spending much of her time visiting her grandchildren in St. Louis, leaving Alice as her father's companion and hostess at the ranch. In his letters, the ever-indulgent Richard would remind Etta to "enjoy yourselves now" and "see that none of Papa's pets wants for anything money will buy," a generosity manifested by numerous drafts on the Mechanics Bank of St. Louis.

During his frequent business trips, Captain King practiced what he preached by spending freely, giving huge tips, and demanding the very best in accommodations and service. On one such trip, he agreed to meet the family at a Galveston hotel, where he found them in the hotel dining room. It seems that a guest and lady friend of Henrietta was having difficulty in cutting a tough piece of meat. Her plight caused Richard to complain first to the waiter, then to the headwaiter. When both failed to respond, the thoroughly riled cowman stormed across the street to another restaurant, where he ordered an entire new meal for the King party; it was to be served at his table in the hotel dining room. A whole troup of waiters delivered the feast, but when they arrived, the hotel waiters refused to clear the King table. Boiling mad by now, the captain yanked the tablecloth from the table, causing food and dishes to fly in all directions. He then carefully respread the tablecloth and ordered the startled hotel waiters to serve the fresh meal — and they did.

Whenever the Kings were in San Antonio, they always stayed at the famed Menger Hotel. Their third-floor rooms faced an ornate balcony overlooking the marble-floored hotel lobby. Once, when Etta was kept waiting after ordering water for the pitcher on her washstand, her impatient husband dropped the empty pitcher over the balcony side, and it crashed on the lobby floor. Leaning over the balustrade, Captain King shouted to the room clerk, "If we can't get any water up here, we don't need a pitcher."

Whenever he was in Brownsville, Richard always bought a round of drinks at Celestin Jagou's saloon before leaving town. He was always a soft touch to anyone

124

there with a sad story, doling out as much as $20 from a roll of smaller bills he kept in a side coat pocket. The captain did, however, keep a close tab on such handouts by recording names and dates. He always left town after dark and traveled on an unannounced road. The larger sums of cash that King kept in an inside coat pocket were often loaned to total strangers. Late one night in San Antonio, he was walking the streets and came upon W. E. Halsell, a cattleman in a bind. Halsell had contracted to buy a herd of steers and put up $10,000 in cash, only to have a local bank renege on a promise to loan the balance of the money. Richard believed his story, and saw that Halsell would make a profit if the deal went through. After introducing himself and shaking hands, Captain King reached into his coat pocket, handed Halsell a wad of large-denomination bills, and told his newfound friend to repay him when the cattle drive was completed. There were no other arrangements, but Richard was later reimbursed every penny of the informal loan.

On the ranch, King could be domineering one minute or "one of the boys" the next. He loved to play pranks on his Kineños and often worked side-by-side with them on sweaty, grimy chores. It was not unusual to find him out with a fence-building crew or working the forge in the blacksmith shop. There was an intense, and reciprocal, bond of loyalty between the captain and his hired hands.[5] No detail of ranch life escaped his watchful eye.

---

[5] In his book *Cow People*, J. Frank Dobie recounts a King Ranch tale about old Ablos. According to Dobie, Ablos was a *caporal* (cow boss) named Ignacio Alvarado, whose father had died protecting Mrs. King during the Civil War. Ignacio was considered the best of all the ranch *caporals* during the days of the great trail drives. One spring in the 1880s, Captain King sent six herds up the trail to Kansas. The last outfit to leave the ranch was delayed several days because Boss Ablos was off on a drinking binge in San Diego. The impatient Richard King II wanted to fire the "old drunkard" on the spot, but his father insisted on waiting a while longer. Sure enough, old Ablos showed up two days later, took over the herd, and left for Kansas. Some three months later, the captain and his son arrived in Dodge City to meet their herds. When they asked their trail bosses how they

When he wanted to tour the ranch, Richard rode the spring seat of a light buckboard hitched to a matching team. Next to his seat was a demijohn of Rose Bud and a Winchester rifle. His driver was Willie Rawlinson, who was brought to the ranch to live when he was an eleven-year-old orphan. Sometimes the two lost their way on the huge ranch, and the captain would say, "Keep driving, Willie, we'll get there all right."

King kept a sharp eye for suspicious strangers and cultivated the image of a man-eater because, as he put it, "If I don't, they'll kill me." Although he made it tough for bandits, rustlers, and hide-peelers on his ranching domain, Richard had a soft spot for "decent men." On one such occasion, he picked up a tired, hungry-looking stranger carrying a gun. When asked why he had not shot a deer or calf, the man replied, "Oh no, I'm on Captain *King's* ranch." The stranger was taken to ranch headquarters, fed, rested, and instructed to kill something for food the next time rather than go hungry.

Since Brownsville was such a long trip from the Santa Gertrudis, King also retained legal counsel at Corpus Christi. He and Mifflin Kenedy brought suit there in 1881 to end a nuisance of trespass by a road crossing their lands. The counsel for the opposition was Robert Justus Kleberg II, a newcomer trying his first case in Nueces County.[6] After winning the case, young Kleberg

made the trip, each offered some excuse for losing cattle en route. Finally, the slow Ablos appeared with his own fat herd, along with 136 "Running W" cattle lost out of the other King outfits. When he heard the good news, a beaming captain turned to young Richard and said, "Now you know why I wait for that old drunkard Ablos."

Some years after King's death, his son-in-law, Robert J. Kleberg, was managing the great ranch and Ablos was still the top *caporal*. After a herd assigned to him was "shaped up" to move out, two days passed and Ablos did not appear to take charge. Then his son rode up to ranch headquarters to report that Ignacio could not come. When pressed for some explanation, young Alvarado replied, "Señor, my father says to bring you his apologies. He says he cannot be at the roundup today, since he has to stay at home to die."

[6] His father, Robert Justus Kleberg I, was born on September 10,

turned in early that night but was awakened by a knock on the door. It was Captain King. Dressed only in a nightshirt, the surprised Robert invited Richard to come in. "I'm looking for a good lawyer. How would a retainer of five thousand a year suit you?" said the cattle baron. Kleberg quickly accepted the offer and rode out to the Santa Gertrudis that very night with his new client.

It was sunup when they reached the ranch house, so the captain awakened nineteen-year-old Alice and asked

---

1803, in Herstelle, Westphalia, Germany. After receiving the degree of doctor juris from the University of Goettingen, he married Rosalie von Roeder in September 1834. Soon thereafter the rest of the von Roeder family joined the newlyweds and sailed for Texas, intent on living under a republican form of government rather than the military despotism of Prussia. After chartering the steamer *Sabine* at New Orleans, the emigrants were shipwrecked on west Galveston Island three days before Christmas, 1834. Another steamer, the *Ocean,* spotted their distress signal and carried the German party to Brazoria. There Kleberg and one of the von Roeders went on foot to San Felipe, where they learned that members of their advance party had located fourteen miles to the southwest at Cat Spring.

After leaving the women and children at Harrisburg, Robert and his companions erected two log houses at Cat Spring, put in ten acres of corn and cotton, then brought their families there. The settlement was so named after Rudolf von Roeder's son shot and killed a Mexican puma at the spring on their farm. The aristocratic Rosalie Kleberg left their furniture, a fine piano (the first one brought to Texas), oil paintings, engravings, music, and books at Harrisburg, all of which was destroyed when General Santa Anna burned the settlement in April 1836.

Upon hearing of the fall of the Alamo, Robert's father-in-law took charge of the family at San Felipe and joined the "Runaway Scrape" in fleeing to safety beyond the Sabine River. Kleberg and two brothers-in-law joined the company of Mosely Baker as privates in the Texas army. The young German judge fought at San Jacinto and was one of three soldiers selected by General Houston to guard the captured Santa Anna. Robert then served in Gen. Thomas Rusk's command, which followed the Mexican army in its retreat beyond the Rio Grande, then gathered the remains of Fannin's massacred men at Goliad and buried them with military honors. When Rusk's company was disbanded, Robert and Rosalie settled at Cat Spring in Austin County.

In 1837 President Houston appointed Kleberg to the Land Commission; he became president of that body a year later. In 1842 Presi-

her to make some coffee. After serving them coffee and sugar cakes in the dining room, Alice peeked through a crack in the door to observe her father discussing business with the young attorney. She later recalled that it was "love at first sight" when she first gazed on the handsome Robert. Ranch legal transactions led to ever-more-frequent visits, and the young couple were soon involved in a very proper, unhurried courtship. On October 2, 1884, Robert sent a letter to Alice's mother, the Victorian manner of asking her daughter's hand in marriage, but no definite wedding plans were made at the time.

In the fall of 1882, Captain King began to suffer severe stomach pains, lost his hearty appetite, and complained of feeling tired much of the time. Only whiskey could dull his relentless stomach ache, and Richard was drinking heavily by the end of the year. The death of his youngest son Lee in early 1883 was a severe emotional blow to the sick cowman. While attending business college at St. Louis, Lee had come down with pneumonia in late February. The entire family was at his bedside when he died on March 1, 1883, in the Southern Hotel. After burying his boy in a St. Louis cemetery, the heartbroken father and Alice returned to the ranch, but Mrs. King remained in the city for months in a state of deep depression. (Lee's body was later moved to San Antonio, then reinterred in the family plot at the Kingsville cemetery.)

---

dent Lamar made Robert a justice of Austin County. After relocating near Meyersville (another German settlement) in 1848, Kleberg became county judge of DeWitt County. During the Civil War he was loyal to the Confederacy, and two sons — Otto and Rudolph — served under Gen. Tom Green in the Confederate army. During his long life Judge Kleberg enjoyed great public esteem. He died at his home near Yorktown on October 23, 1888, and was buried in the family cemetery. Kleberg County was named in his honor in 1913.

Robert Justus II, the youngest of his four sons, was born on the family farm near Meyersville on December 5, 1853. After receiving a degree from the University of Virginia law school in 1880, he joined the law firm of Stayton & Lackey at Cuero, then moved to the branch office at Corpus Christi, where Richard King became one of his clients.

The toll taken by his physical and emotional ordeal is revealed in a letter Richard wrote Etta on April 8, 1883. "I am tired of this business, as I at all times have made a mess of everything that I have undertaken . . . and now I want to quit the Rancho business and will do so," said the heartsick husband.

Preoccupied with Lee's death, Captain King did not trail any herds north in the spring of 1883. Two other factors also contributed to his overstocked pastures and the need to sell off some herds. Starting in 1881, barbed wire fences had limited access to the old trail drive routes. At the same time, Longhorns carrying the dreaded "Texas Fever" to northern herds were being turned back by "Winchester Quarantines." It was during this period that the value of Texas rangeland increased as English and Scottish speculators and investors sought new profits in Western ranching. In early 1882, Mifflin Kenedy received $1.1 million for his Los Laureles ranch from a syndicate in Dundee, Scotland, the Texas Land & Cattle Co., Ltd. Within a month he made his La Parra grant the headquarters of a new ranching property, the Kenedy Pasture Company, and moved his family to Corpus Christi.

By the spring of 1883, King was negotiating to sell the Santa Gertrudis to a British syndicate through their agent, a Mr. Hancock. As reported by the *New Orleans Times Democrat,* the asking price for the ranch and its stock was $6.5 million. Evidently, it was the sheer magnitude of the King *rancho* that caused the transaction to collapse. When Hancock and his buyers visited the ranch between mid-April and late June 1883, the British party asked to see the cattle first. Richard ordered a roundup in Preso de las Tranquitas, and Ramón Alvarado brought in about 12,000 head for their inspection at 9:00 one morning. The British buyers were shocked to hear Captain King express disappointment that such a little herd had been gathered. When Richard matter-of-factly remarked that he could bring in *four* or *five* herds equal to this one, an awed buyer said he had seen enough, that they couldn't afford even the herd they had inspected, much less the land. Once this sale fell through, King never mentioned quitting ranching again.

Rains ended a prolonged South Texas drought in July 1883, prompting the gaunt captain to write his wife, "We are all well and the grass in the yard is green once more, thanks be to God for it." When Richard II was engaged to Pearl Ashbrook that summer, his father gave him the 40,000-acre Rancho Puerta de Agua Dulce as a wedding gift on July 15. The couple were married in Wentzville, Missouri, at the home of Pearl's grandmother on December 12, 1883. Once Richard II set up his own Agua Dulce ranching operation, he began to convert some grazing pastures to farmlands and introduced cotton-growing. Now, only Alice King was left at home. Despite her valiant but vain effort to stop his hard drinking, an appreciative father could write, "She is a little lady in all things and so good I could not do without my little Pet . . ."

King put herds on the trail north again in 1884. The fall found Walter Billingsley in Cheyenne, Wyoming, with 5,600 King ranch steers. At Fort Sidney, Nebraska, he showed a local banker his 150 saddle horses and branded herd before making out a bank draft. The sight of the renowned "Running W" brand was all the banker required in the way of identification from a total stranger.

During November 17–22, 1884, Captain King attended the first — and last — National Stockmen's Convention meeting in the Exposition Building at St. Louis. Among the 1,365 certified delegates were 300 Texans, including King, Shanghai Pierce, and Charles Goodnight. At the time, they had a million head of cattle to be marketed. Their old cattle trails were either being fenced out of existence or closed by Winchester quarantines of their disease-carrying Longhorns. To the beleaguered Texas cattlemen, there was a simple solution to their plight: the creation of an official cattle trail. Such an idea was first conceived by King, who proposed that the cowmen organize a corporation and purchase the land needed for the cattle strip. Since it would be privately owned and controlled, such a trail would not be a hostage to periodic political whims. Richard's bold approach was opposed, however, by a majority of the delegates, who insisted that the federal government should donate public domain just as it had earlier granted big tracts for railroad construction.

Once the convention organized, Judge Carroll of Denton, Texas, made an eloquent opening speech defending the Texas proposal. He ended with a motion that the convention, in its first official act, memorialize the U.S. Congress to establish a National Cattle Trail extending north-northwest from the Red River to the Canadian border. The full convention adopted such a resolution and appointed a committee of nine to make specific recommendations for the proposed national trail. This committee suggested that such a fenced, grassy corridor should be 690 miles long and from three to six miles wide. The nine pointed out that the total area of the trail, all of it government land, would be 1,324,800 acres, only 2.78 percent of the land the federal government had granted Western railroads.

After the convention adjourned, Congressman James F. Miller of Galveston introduced a bill authorizing the U.S. secretary of the interior to appoint three committees to lay out and establish a national cattle trail. Senator Richard Coke of Texas introduced a companion bill in the U.S. Senate, but Congress adjourned without taking any action on the plan. Initially, such indifference to their plight led Texas cattlemen to bluster about creating such a cattle trail by force, using Texas Rangers as escorts on the cattle drives. It was apparent, however, that no one wanted — or needed — the trail except the Texans, and the movement soon ended with the death of its driving force, Richard King.

When Old Cap returned to the Santa Gertrudis from St. Louis, he was fighting a losing battle with a relentless foe, stomach cancer. His black hair and beard had turned iron gray, he had an ashened complexion, and his clothes hung on a rail-thin frame. Gulps of whiskey now brought only temporary relief from the incessant pain. However, the melancholy mood of the family was brightened by the birth of Richard King III on December 17, 1884.

Barely making it home from a Corpus Christi business trip on January 13, 1885, the mortally ill captain was confined to the ranch for a month. Etta and Alice finally convinced Richard to put himself under the care of Dr. Ferdinand Herff at San Antonio. When he left the Santa Gertrudis for good on February 25, he had to be helped to the big coach bound for Collins Station. After a final round of handshakes with the assembled Kineños and their families, Captain King departed with the tearful cry *"Ádiós patrón!"* ringing in his ears.

Even as he faced death, the legendary rancher was thinking of the future. His last instructions for attorney Jim Wells were, "Tell him to keep on buying [lands in the San Juan de Carricitos] . . . and not to let a foot of dear old Santa Gertrudis get away from us." Richard King left behind ranch holdings totaling 614,140 acres, 40,000 branded head of cattle, 6,600 horses, and 12,000 sheep and goats.[7] By this time, the King Ranch was so vast that it took a man on horseback a week to circle his fences.

---

[7] The horse business was always profitable on the King Ranch. The first ranch receipts involved the sale of horses and mules. In 1854 the captain paid $1,100 for a gray stallion, a bay stallion, and a sorrel stud. His best stock was systematically infused with the blood of quality studs. Among his best horses were the iron grays, and one such stud is the source of a great story.

On May 12, 1875, a stagecoach was robbed between Austin and San Antonio. The highwaymen entertained the passengers with wisecracks during the holdup, a technique often employed by the notorious James-Younger gang. Later that month a stranger riding a beautiful iron gray stallion rode up to the Santa Gertrudis commissary and asked to spend the night. Captain King happened to be nearby and gazed admiringly at the magnificent horse before showing the visitor to the bunkhouse. When the horseman left at first light, Richard assigned a *vaquero* to take him to the San Antonio road. Just when his guide was about to turn back, the stranger said, "Get down. I want to change with you. Take this horse back to Capt. King and tell him that Jesse James sent him as a gift with his compliments." Such a stunt

Soon after Richard reached the Menger Hotel in San Antonio, Dr. Herff diagnosed his condition as terminal stomach cancer, news the patient calmly received. All of the family, along with Robert Kleberg and Mifflin Kenedy, gathered for the death watch. Although Kenedy was still mourning the recent loss of both his wife Petra and son James, the lifelong friend kept a vigil at King's bedside and telegraphed for specialists from New Orleans, but it was too late. When Dr. Herff commented that his patient's Rose Bud whiskey would only hasten his death, Etta King implored the physician to see if Richard would give up the drinking she so despised, to "tell him with a smile that I need him a while longer." Once Dr. Herff passed on Etta's appeal, the captain never touched another drink.

On April 2, 1885, the famed cowman directed the making of his will, leaving all of an estate valued at $1,061,484 to Henrietta King to be used and disposed of as she pleased. At dusk on the evening of April 14, the sixty-year-old King quietly departed this life, surrounded by family and friends. The next day, funeral services were held at 4:30 P.M. in the parlor of the Menger Hotel. A long cortege then moved to the San Antonio city cemetery. Reverend J. W. Neil, pastor of the First Presbyterian Church, presided at the graveside services.

The death of Richard King was noted by newspapers throughout the United States. One Texas paper observed that "his history is almost a history of this frontier." Perhaps the most credible tribute came from a contemporary, old Rip Ford, who later wrote:

> . . . He possessed financial ability of the first order, and he amassed a fortune . . . upon a theater of action where many failed . . . [He was] a pioneer settler who

---

would have been in character for the infamous outlaw; after all, he was known as a connoisseur of horses and loved a good — and surprising — joke. This gift horse sired a line of big, strong, fine-limbed offspring known as "Jesse James horses."

133

stepped to the front, jeopardizing life and property, and who became instrumental in opening up thousands of square miles to settlement. The ranch of Santa Gertrudis became the center around which civilization clustered . . . where Captain King introduced the arts of peace, . . .

This story would not be complete without further reference to the legacy of Captain King. The ranching empire he created was managed by a succession of Klebergs after 1886. Shortly after returning home, the widow King appointed her daughter's fiancé, Robert Kleberg, as ranch manager. She gave him few instructions, preferring to tell Robert that "you know best." The thirty-one-year-old lawyer was faced with a crash course in mastering every detail of practical ranching. Kleberg was literally on trial before 300 ranch employees, who referred to their new patron as "El Abogado" (the lawyer). His first order of business was selling off some 20,000 acres of odd parcels to pay off ranch debts, a situation caused by the captain's incessant land purchases. Within ten years the last debts of the estate were cleared from the books. There were no cattle drives after King's death; instead, ranch livestock were shipped to market on nearby rails.

In June 1886, Robert Kleberg married Alice King in a small, private ceremony at the Santa Gertrudis ranch house, and his mother-in-law accompanied the couple north on their honeymoon. When they returned home late that summer and set up housekeeping in the old rambling frame ranch house, Henrietta's bedroom was directly across the hall from that of the newlyweds. Even after the old place burned in 1912, and Robert built a grand *hacienda* (the present Big House), the same living arrangement continued.

For decades Mrs. King continued to be "the *boss* wherever she was" on a domain referred to as "the widow's ranch." She always presided at the family dinner table, where her standards of propriety made no allowance for shirt-sleeve dining. Thus the Kleberg men

134

sweated through meals while dressed in wool trousers and coats, stiff collars, and high boots. Many of the ranch house rooms had large portraits of Etta's deceased husband. As pioneer, founder, and owner, she expected — and demanded — her just due. The often-ailing matriarch always dressed in severe black and made a grand tour of the *rancho* twice a year in her heavy black Rockaway stagecoach. Whether at the dinner table or in a rocking chair on an outside gallery, the widow King was very free with advice on how to raise the five Kleberg children, who grew up on the ranch. Although the two boys and three girls attended school in Corpus Christi, a ranch stagecoach picked them up every Friday at the Collins Station train stop.

In 1891, Robert Kleberg built the world's first cattle dipping vat, using an arsenical solution that killed the blood-sucking cattle ticks that transmitted Texas Fever. Two years later he introduced Hereford and Shorthorn cattle to the King Ranch. His early experiments with demonstration farming marked the beginning of the South Texas citrus industry. It was Robert's ultimate dream to civilize the arid region with towns, farms, and schools following in the wake of a proposed new railroad from Corpus Christi to Brownsville. Such a transformation required an adequate water supply, so Robert began an intense search for deep artesian wells on the ranch. On June 6, 1899, a Nebraska company using new deep-drilling equipment struck water at 532 feet some five miles northwest of present Kingsville. Kleberg cried when he saw that first well. Soon seventy-five such artesian wells eliminated the water problem, and 225 windmills dotted the ranch landscape, each serving an individual pasture.

Although his water supply was assured, Robert was rejected when he asked the Southern Pacific Railroad to extend its lines from Alice to Brownsville in 1902. He then contacted B. F. Yoakum, president of the Frisco Railroad, in St. Louis, and offered to donate ranch land for a railroad right-of-way. Yoakum sent veteran builder Uriah Lott to meet Kleberg and survey a suitable rail route, while the Frisco executive organized a syndicate of ninety-nine members who would own all the capital stock and bonds in the St. Louis, Brownsville & Mexico Railroad.[8] This new line was incorporated on January 12, 1903, with Lott as president and Kleberg as vice-president. On July 28, 1903, the first track was laid in Robert Driscoll's pasture at present Robstown.

---

[8] Uriah Lott, the promoter and president of three South Texas railroads, was born in Albany, New York, on January 30, 1842. After learning to grade wool and hides, he moved in 1869 from Brownsville to Corpus Christi, where he opened a commission business. In 1871 Uriah established a regular line of three sailing ships to transport wool and hides from Corpus Christi to New York.

In March 1875 a charter was taken out for the Corpus Christi, San Diego & Rio Grande Narrow Gauge Railroad, with Lott as president. Mifflin Kenedy subscribed the first $10,000, while Richard King's pledge of $30,000 was used to buy the line's first locomotive. Colonel Lott drove the first gilded spike near the Corpus Christi waterfront on Thanksgiving Day, 1876, and the first twenty-five miles of the railroad were put in operation in January 1877. Although sixteen sections of State land were granted for every mile of track built, these lands brought only $10 a section, forcing Uriah to wage a constant, desperate battle for funds. Additional aid from King and Kenedy made it possible to continue the line twenty-seven miles to San Diego in March 1879. Unable to raise more local capital, Lott and Kenedy traveled to New York, where they persuaded the Palmer-Sullivan Syndicate, builders of the Mexican National Railway, to acquire the assets of their company. In June 1881 the syndicate obtained a new charter, and the name of "Lott's Folly" was changed to the Texas Mexican Railway Company. With ample funds thus assured, the road was completed to Laredo in November 1881.

Uriah's second rail venture, the San Antonio and Aransas Pass Railway, was begun 1884. After the line built from San Antonio to Floresville in 1886, Lott became discouraged, and Mifflin Kenedy took over the contract to build the road, taking his payment in stocks, bonds, and bonuses. He reached Houston in 1888, but the line was forced into receivership in July 1890, with Lott's S.A.A.P. properties slipping from his hands. Receivers B. F. Yoakum and J. S. McNamara authorized Kenedy to complete the line between Lexington and Lott. Within a year he finished the road, laying a total of 688 miles of main line track in five years. The new railroad gave San Antonio a gulf out-

One day Robert and his mother-in-law rode from the remote ranch house to the shady spot where Captain King had first spread a blanket for roundup picnics. According to family legend, he remarked, "Here, we will build our town." In January 1903 Mrs. King deeded 41,820 acres to the Kleberg Town and Improvement Company, a stock company that would sell farm and town sites. Within this area a site of 853 acres was surveyed to form the town of Kingsville. The new town was born on July 4, 1904, when two shiny new trains — one southbound and one northbound — pulled into the depot. From the beginning, Kingsville was the nerve center for the St. Louis, Brownsville & Mexico Railroad (now part of the Missouri-Pacific system). It was a terminal for trains and enginemen, and general offices were located there. Situated in the heart of the King Ranch, the new town became the county seat of newly organized Kleberg County in 1913.

With Mrs. King's backing, Robert established the city waterworks, a power company, an ice and milling company, a newspaper, a lumber company, a bank, and a cotton oil and spinning mill. He also built nearly all the cotton gins between Corpus Christi and Brownsville. His mother-in-law built the Henrietta M. King High School, the Presbyterian Church, and donated the land for every other church in town.

Ninety-two-year-old Henrietta King died at the Santa Gertrudis on March 31, 1925. After her body lay in state in the front room of the great *hacienda,* her simple

---

let and created the new townsites of Kenedy and Yoakum. Since 1925, the San Antonio and Aransas Pass Railway has been a part of the Southern Pacific system.

Colonel Lott's most successful promotion was the St. Louis, Brownsville & Mexican Railroad, incorporated in January 1903 with himself as president. He personally conducted Train No. 1 out of Corpus Christi on July 4, 1904, and was greeted by 600 residents at Brownsville. Sadly, the ailing promoter spent his last years in poverty as a guest of the King family at Hotel Ricardo in Kingsville. He died lonely and forgotten at age seventy-three on March 29, 1915, and was buried beside his wife Cicele in Chamberlain Park.

funeral was held there on April 4. An honor guard of almost 200 Kineños led a mile-long cortege to the Kingsville cemetery, which Henrietta had planted and named Chamberlain Park in honor of her father. When the casket was lowered into the ground, the Kineños circled the open grave on horseback at a fast canter, hats by their side, in a final salute to La Patrona. That fall the remains of Captain King, son Lee, and daughter Ella were brought to Kingsville from San Antonio and reinterred at her side. They rest there together under a shaft of granite with the simple inscription: KING.

When the widow died in 1925, the ranch was divided among her heirs. The children of Richard King, Jr., and Nettie Atwood received the Santa Fe and El Sauz ranches, respectively, while Robert and Alice Kleberg inherited 825,000 acres of the ranch. Mrs. King's will stipulated that Robert Kleberg, Jr., would serve as trustee of the estate for ten years. In 1934 the King Ranch became a private corporation owned by the Klebergs and their five children.

During Robert Kleberg's long stint as manager, the ranch doubled in size to 1.2 million acres. Among his land acquisitions was the Laureles Ranch, purchased from Scots who had bought it from Mifflin Kenedy. After the onset of palsy limited his activities, his second son, Robert (Bob) Kleberg, Jr., came home to run the ranch in 1918 after spending two years studying agriculture at the University of Wisconsin. The elder Kleberg died at the King Ranch headquarters on October 10, 1932; he and wife Alice lie beside Captain and Mrs. King in Chamberlain Cemetery.

Bob Kleberg was more earnest and serious than his dashing older brother, Richard Mifflin, who served in the U.S. Congress from 1932 until 1944, and gave Lyndon Johnson his first job in Washington. After taking on the full-time responsibility of running the King Ranch in 1919, "Mr. Bob" moved out of the Big House his father had built in 1912 and into a modest-but-comfortable

Cape Cod bungalow next door. Bob's wife Helen, who persuaded him to establish a thoroughbred racing stable on the ranch in 1935, served as the model for Leslie Benedict in the movie *Giant*. The King Ranch was to produce two famous thoroughbreds: "Assault" won the Triple Crown of racing in 1946, while "Middleground" won both the Kentucky Derby and the Belmont in 1950.

Among Bob Kleberg's ranch inventions were the cattle prod and a root plow driven by a huge bulldozer, used to clear mesquite brush below the surface. He also engineered the deal with Humble Oil and Refining Company for the ranch's oil and gas rights in 1933, at that time the largest lease in the world. In 1958 a new agreement extended the Humble lease. In June 1969 an article in *Fortune* magazine estimated the yearly ranch revenues from oil and gas royalties at $15–18 million — fifteen times the profits of ranch operations. As of 1980 there were 2,730 oil and gas wells on the ranch. Between 1946 and 1970, Kleberg used oil money to add eight million acres to ranch operations through long-term land leases both in the States (Kentucky, Pennsylvania, Florida, and Mississippi) and abroad (Australia, Cuba, Brazil, Argentina, Venezuela, Morocco, and Spain).

"Mr. Bob" also developed the first American breed of cattle and a new ranch quarter horse. Starting his breeding experimentation in 1910, he produced the Santa Gertrudis through generations of crossing Brahman bulls with pure-bred English Shorthorn cows. When the bull calf "Monkey" (so named due to his playful antics) was born in 1920, he was technically three-eighths Brahman and five-eighths Shorthorn. Monkey was deep russet in color, long and well-proportioned, and combined the hardiness of the Brahman with the temperament and beef qualities of the fat, docile Shorthorn. The Santa Gertrudis cow was impervious to insects and disease, a prolific breeder, and could thrive on heat and South Texas range conditions. It was officially recognized as a new breed by the U.S. Department of Agriculture in 1940.

Kleberg began a quarterhorse breeding program in the early 1920s. The father of the new line was a stallion named "Old Sorrel," a deep red ranch horse Bob described as "a joy to ride." When the American Quarter Horse Association was founded in 1941, the King Ranch stallion "Wimpy P-1" was given the first number in the stud book. These King Ranch quarter horses are compact, nimble, have unusual stamina, and are superior cow horses. Over 2,000 of them are used on the ranch today, and they have been purchased by Ringling Brothers for their circus acts. Every October the ranch auctions off selected Santa Gertrudis cattle and quarter horses.

Helen Kleberg died in June 1963. Shortly before Bob's death, he told his six grandchildren, "Do what you can with the ranch but, above all, keep the family together." When he died in a Houston hospital on October 13, 1974, at age seventy-eight, "Mr. Bob" was both president and general manager of the King Ranch.

Beginning in 1974, James H. Clement served as president and chief executive officer of King Ranch, Inc. for thirteen years. In June 1987 he was elected chairman of the board and was succeeded by John B. Armstrong. Elected as vice-president was Stephen J. "Tio" Kleberg, a great-great-grandson of Captain King, who is general manager of the South Texas operations of the King Ranch. For the first time in its history, the King Ranch, Inc. board of directors in November 1987 elected three new board members who are not blood relatives or in-laws of either Richard King or his son-in-law, Robert Justus Kleberg II. President Armstrong stated that the outsiders — corporation chief executives from Dallas and Chicago — would bring "greater insight and diversity of experience to the board." The election took place in the great *hacienda* built by Robert Kleberg in 1912, which is now used only for guests, special occasions, and annual family business meetings.

Today the four South Texas divisions of the King

Ranch cover 825,000 acres, an area much larger than the state of Rhode Island. The Santa Gertrudis, Laureles, Encino, and Norias divisions are encircled by 2,000 miles of wire-mesh fence. The ranch is home to 60,000 head of cattle and a sophisticated feed mill and feedlot capable of fattening 20,000 cattle at a time. The ranch also contains one of the largest farms in South Texas, with 37,400 acres planted in cotton and milo.

Such is the monument to — and legacy of — a young Irish steamboater who waded ashore in Texas in 1847, with only a seabag in hand.

Richard King
— Courtesy Perry-Castañeda
Library, The University of
Texas at Austin

Henrietta M. King (1871)
— Courtesy John A. Cypher,
Jr., King Ranch, Inc.

The King family
— Courtesy John A. Cypher, Jr., King Ranch, Inc.

The Partners: Richard King (seated) and Mifflin Kenedy.
— Courtesy King Ranch, Inc.

Henrietta M. King and Robert J. Kleberg, Sr., inspecting one of the first artesian wells on the King Ranch.
— Courtesy John A. Cypher, Jr., King Ranch, Inc.

An engagement picture of
Alice G. King and Robert J.
Kleberg.

— Courtesy King Ranch, Inc.

Bob Kleberg cuts a Santa
Gertrudis yearling out of a
King Ranch herd.

— Courtesy John A. Cypher,
Jr., King Ranch, Inc.

Robert J. Kleberg, Jr. (1896–1974)
— Courtesy John A. Cypher, Jr.,
King Ranch, Inc.

"Monkey," the sire of the Santa Gertrudis cattle breed.
— Courtesy John A. Cypher, Jr., King Ranch, Inc.

Governor Beauford Jester and Congressman Richard Mifflin Kleberg admire the King Ranch Triple Crown winner, "Assault."
— Courtesy John A. Cypher, Jr., King Ranch, Inc.

A cattle train loading on the King Ranch.
— Courtesy John A. Cypher, Jr., King Ranch, Inc.

The Santa Gertrudis "Big House" at the time Kingsville was founded. The structure burned in 1912.

— Courtesy John A. Cypher, Jr., King Ranch, Inc.

The Main House at King Ranch

— Courtesy King Ranch, Inc.

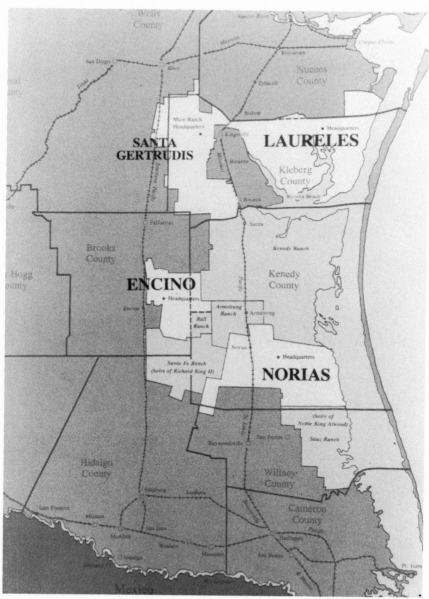

A map showing locations of the four divisions of King Ranch.
— Courtesy King Ranch, Inc.

147

IV

Sul Ross:
Warrior, Public Servant, and Educator

When he died in 1898, a tribute by the *Dallas Morning News* included this statement: "It has been the lot of few men to be of such great service to Texas as Sul Ross ..." He came from good stock: his father, Shapley P. Ross, was a renowned frontier fighter, Indian agent, and a founder of Waco. Sul first gained fame as the gallant young Ranger captain who bested the fierce Comanches and rescued Cynthia Ann Parker. His Civil War exploits as a scout and raider won him the rank of Confederate brigadier general at age twenty-five. Starting from scratch after the war, Sul became a prosperous farmer and cattleman, the sheriff of McLennan County, a drafter of the Texas Constitution of 1876, state senator, two-term governor of Texas, and president of Texas A&M College. Indeed, giving credibility to that struggling school was his crowning achievement. This fearless soldier and authentic hero was also a devoted husband and father, and a learned man who valued spiritual and cultural ideals. Modest and unassuming by nature, Ross stood for spotless integrity, rigid honesty, and balanced common sense as a public servant.

Shapley Prince Ross was born on the family farm

near Louisville, Kentucky, in 1811. When Shapley was six his father moved the family to Jackson in Lincoln County, Missouri, where the boy grew up and experienced only six months of formal schooling. After working in the Galena lead mines and racing and dealing in blooded horses, Ross used his earnings to buy a farm. When he was nineteen, Shapley married Catherine Fulkerson, the pampered daughter of a rich German planter from St. Charles County, in November 1830. After a year on the farm and a brief stay at Troy, Missouri, the couple settled in the new town of Bentonsport, Iowa Territory, near a reservation of Sauk and Fox Indians in 1834. For some four years Shapley traded with the Indians and operated a hotel in town.

Shortly after their fourth child, Lawrence Sullivan, was born on September 27, 1838, the cold climate forced the Ross family back to St. Charles County, Missouri. In early 1839 a traveler told Shapley of the boundless opportunities in the Republic of Texas. Ignoring dire warnings from relatives about the dangers and lack of schools there, the hardy pioneers struck out for Texas that fall and camped at Waco Springs en route to the Robertson Colony town of Old Nashville on the lower Brazos.

Two years later, the Rosses were one of eight families who joined Capt. Daniel Monroe, who owned a league of land near present Cameron. After receiving a 640-acre headright, Shapley set to work clearing 130 acres of good farm land. The Monroe settlement intruded on the Comanche range and faced constant danger from marauding Indians, so the Ross boys grew up familiar with both ax and rifle. When Lawrence Sullivan (or "Sul," as he preferred) was just a toddler, he and his pa walked a mile to visit a neighbor. On their way home a war party of fifteen mounted Comanches gave chase. Shapley swept up his son, piggy-back style, and made a moonlight dash over the open prairie to the safety of their cabin. Since neither was hit by the barrage of arrows, the boy was told not to worry his mother with news of the close call, but little Sul blurted out, "Whew, Papa, didn't we fairly fly?"

Captain Ross worked his farm for a year before his first Indian fight. After ransacking the camp of George B. Erath and his surveying party, five Comanche raiders followed the trail to the Monroe settlement and stole all of their horses that night. The next morning the men gave chase after borrowing the mules of an itinerant trader named Wilson. Thinking that they were safe, the Comanches took their time retreating, enabling Shapley and the others to catch up with them on Boggy Creek near present Georgetown. All five warriors were killed, and Ross used his Bowie knife to dispatch the notorious Chief Bigfoot in hand-to-hand combat. All the horses were recovered, along with the buckskin britches of Erath, which the Indians had stuffed with corn.

A short time later, thirty Comanche warriors surrounded the Ross cabin while Shapley was lying ill on the porch. The braves had surprised and captured Sul while he was resting on a quilt, then dragged their hostage to the cabin. The old chief informed the senior Ross that he would make a treaty after young Sul led his hungry warriors to the corn and melon fields. Frontier boys wore only a single "warmus," a shirt reaching the ankles, so when Sul trotted off toward the fields, the Comanches whipped his bare legs with their arrow shafts. Young Ross refused to flinch or show signs of pain or fear. He returned with both legs bleeding, but the Indians were so impressed by his bravery that they made a peace treaty with Shapley.

From time to time Captain Ross joined Jack Hays and his Ranger company in campaigns against the Indians. In 1843 Hays commissioned him to take an escort of sixteen men into Mexico and gather information about the Mier prisoners. Ross and his party were gone fifty-seven days on this successful mission but had to resort to eating horse meat to avoid starvation. While their dad was away, Sul and older brother Peter were left in charge of the Cameron farm.

In 1845 the Ross family moved to Austin so that the four oldest children could attend a one-room school. After trading 290 acres of land to Captain Monroe for a wagon and yoke of oxen, Shapley took what possessions he could carry along with the slave Armstead. When the older city boys gave seven-year-old Sul a hard time about his frontier "warmus," he jumped on his largest antagonist and put him on the ground as his proud father looked on. While Captain Ross and his Ranger company were off protecting the frontier during the Mexican War, his family remained in Austin.

In early 1849, land developer Jacob de Cordova offered Shapley four free lots in Waco, the new town he was laying off at the historic crossroad where the Brazos meets the Bosque. As further enducement Ross was given the right to operate the ferry across the Brazos and to buy up to eighty acres of rich farm bottomland at $1.25 an acre. That March the Ross family moved to Waco, built the first house there — a double log cabin on a bluff above the springs — and got in a spring crop. Daughter Kate was the first white child born in Waco. In addition to running the ferry, Shapley built the first hotel in Waco on Bridge Street, managed the city waterworks, and trailed cattle to Missouri. He was also a regular at the local horse races, with Sul serving as the family jockey.

Even as a boy, young Ross showed a reckless, fearless streak. After Indian raiders stole his favorite mount and other horses, Sul and the slave Armstead mounted a mule and joined the pursuing posse without his father's permission. The slower animal could not keep up with the chase, however, and all the frustrated Sul got for his efforts was a tongue-lashing from his dad. It seems that Mrs. Ross, a Waco schoolmistress, was always fretting about her boy's drinking, profanity, and combative nature; indeed, he was prone to violence with the potential for going "bad" until education and religion gave Sul some needed self-control.

In March 1856, the seventeen-year-old Ross enrolled for the new term in the Preparatory Department of Baylor University at Independence. The university catalogue required that his moral character be assessed through an interview with President Rufus C. Burleson, and several factors weighed against his candidacy: He was two years older than the recommended age for admission; his mother was a Roman Catholic; his violent-tempered father was indifferent to formal religion. The Baylor president saw his potential, however, and accepted Sul as a new student. Sul immediately sold his horse and equipment to help pay college expenses and signed a statement indicating his willingness to submit to the restrictive university rules.

Determined to be at the head of his classes, Ross received no demerits as he raced through the two-year course of study required for entry to college-level courses in only nine months. The impressed Burleson described Sul as an excellent student noted for "modesty, firmness, good nature, a clear well-balanced mind, and devotion to duty," going so far as to tell him, "You will be governor of Texas some day, and I will vote for you."

During the 1856 school year, Baylor and the pastor of the Independence Baptist Church sponsored a revival which all students were encouraged to attend. Sul was under conviction and went to the services every night. Before the meeting was over, Burleson said that he "saw and joyfully embraced the plan of salvation." This conversion experience had a profound influence on the former ruffian, although Ross did not join a church until two years later. For some unknown reason, Sul chose to leave Baylor at the end of the year and transferred to Wesleyan University in Florence, Alabama, the oldest college in the state.

The 180 male students of Wesleyan stayed with prominent local families rather than live in dormitories.

Therefore, they had daily exposure to good manners and refinement. When Ross enrolled in 1857, the examining board found him deficient in math and required that he spend a year in the Preparatory Department. The disappointed newcomer thought of returning to Texas, but then a kindly professor, Septimus P. Rice, agreed to board Sul in his home and to tutor him in math at night. By concentrating on courses in mathematics and the classics, young Ross was able to pass exams admitting him to college studies by the end of his first session.

During his stay at Florence, he joined the Methodist Episcopal Church South, made numerous campus and town friends, and evolved from a rough, hotheaded frontiersman to a cool planter gentleman. When the university term ended on July 7, 1858, Sul returned to Texas for a summer break that brought him acclaim as an Indian fighter.

In 1854 the Texas legislature had passed a bill authorizing land for two Indian reservations. On September 1, 1855, Captain Shapley Ross was appointed as agent of the eight-square-league Brazos Agency some ten miles below Fort Belknap. This Lower Reserve was for the twelve "sedentary" or agricultural tribes, including the Caddo, Waco, Tonkawa, Tawakoni, Keechi, and Delaware Indians. To protect these peaceful tribes, the federal government stationed two companies at both the Second Dragoons and the Seventh Infantry at nearby Fort Belknap. Some hundred of these agency braves enlisted as scouts and trackers for forays against the hated, feared Comanches, who frequently raided frontier settlements from their smaller reservation on the Clear Fork of the Brazos.

On April 22, 1858, Texas Ranger Captain "Rip" Ford led a force north from Fort Belknap on a reprisal raid against the Comanches. His 102 Rangers were joined by Captain Ross and 111 Tonkawa scouts under Chief Placido, reservation Indians who were loyal to their agent.

After crossing the Red River on April 29, Ford's men spotted fresh Indian signs at the mouth of the Washita.

Early on the morning of May 12, they attacked a Comanche village of 400 warriors on a fork of the Canadian River. This was the encampment of Chief Pohebits Quasho (or Iron Jacket), who considered himself invincible because he wore an ancient Spanish coat of mail. When the Battle of Antelope Hills began, the chief pranced in front of the skirmish line hurling challenges to the whites. After Iron Jacket was killed early on by a heavy Tonkawa bullet, his demoralized braves fled and were routed during a five-mile fight. At 1:00, however, Captain Ford saw an approaching division of 500 fresh warriors led by second-in-command Chief Peta Nacona. A series of individual challenges and jousts followed between the Comanches and Tonkawas before Nacona's braves were defeated and forced to retreat by Ford's superior firepower. During this all-day battle, the Comanches lost 75 warriors and 475 horses; only two Rangers were killed, and Ross had no reservation Indian casualties. This total Texan victory was celebrated that night when the Tonkawas feasted on the severed hands and feet of the hated Comanches.

By the time Sul reached Waco in the summer of 1858, a two-story house was going up on the Ross family farm south of town. Hearing that a regular army campaign was shaping up against Comanche Chief Buffalo Hump, and that his father's agency Indians were to fight again as auxiliaries, young Ross rushed to the Brazos Reserve in Young County. Shapley was hoping to lead his Indians again but was not feeling well at the time. When the reservation chiefs saw the nineteen-year-old college student ride in, they chose him as their war leader. His proud father concurred.

On September 13, 1858, Sul and his 135 Caddo and Delaware Indians joined regular army forces at Fort Belknap. This major offensive was to be led by Bvt. Maj. Earl Van Dorn, a dashing Mississippian commanding four companies of the Second Cavalry and a detachment from the First Infantry, making a total force of some 300 men. On the fifteenth, Van Dorn's force headed northwest toward Indian Territory, with Sul's Indians riding ahead as scouts. Ross's men reached Otter Creek on the twenty-third and set up a base camp near present Tipton, Oklahoma. When Van Dorn arrived three days later, he built a stockade called Camp Radziminski. On September 29, some Delaware scouts reported finding Buffalo Hump and a large Comanche camp near a Wichita village on the banks of Rush Creek. The tribe was trading, gambling, and feasting with the Comanches. Neither feared an attack in Indian Territory.

Although the scouts estimated the Comanche camp to be forty miles away, the distance was actually closer to ninety miles. Leaving his infantry behind as guards, Van Dorn's cavalry and Sul's Indians began a forced march within the hour, hoping to attack at dawn the next day. When daybreak came, however, there was no Comanche camp in sight, so Earl's forces continued to ride all day, eating jerked beef in the saddle. When they finally rested at sunset, the troopers had ridden continuously for sixteen and a half hours. After dark a Caddo scout brought word of the Comanche camp, and Van Dorn's men positioned themselves as close as possible during the cold night.

Just before sunup on October 1, 1858, the pursuers reached a rolling prairie bounded by a series of ridges to the north, with the Comanche camp in a valley just beyond. While the army troops undertook a company front attack in four columns, Ross charged the upper end of the village and drove off the Comanche pony herd, thus forcing the enemy to fight on foot. Hidden by thick fog, the 225 army troopers advanced on the lower end of a Comanche camp caught by total surprise. For two hours the warriors fought hand-to-hand among the 120 lodges of the strung-out village, then fled to the sheltering banks of the numerous ravines.

Once he stampeded the Comanche herd, Sul rode back

to the chaotic camp and gave chase to a large group of fleeing women and children. With the help of one Caddo and two troopers, he managed to cut off and herd the fugitives together. Realizing that an eight-year-old was a white girl, Ross shouted, "Grab her," to the Caddo scout.[1] Suddenly, the four men found themselves separated from the main force by twenty-five Comanche warriors. The two troopers were killed during the sudden attack, while Sul was wounded in the shoulder by an arrow, then shot off his horse by the heavy slug of a captured .58-caliber Springfield carbine. The bullet ripped through his chest and partially paralyzed his side. Just as the prone Ross tried to draw his revolver with his other hand, he recognized his assailant as being sub-chief Mohee, a warrior who had often visited Fort Belknap. Mohee drew his butcher knife to scalp Sul but was suddenly called away by his leader; as he bounded off, Mohee was killed by a carbine shot from Lt. James P. Major. Indeed, this was an extremely close brush with death for Ross, who later remarked, "For their services Major Van Dorn gave the Indians of my command the captured spoils. I received for my pay a dangerous gunshot wound . . ."

The Battle of Wichita Village was a complete victory over the Comanches; while Van Dorn had four losses, the enemy suffered seventy dead and all their lodges and supplies were put to the torch. Although Buffalo Hump and two-thirds of his warriors escaped, they left 300 animals behind. Major Van Dorn suffered a severe arrow wound to his upper stomach and left lung, and Captain Ross was so critically wounded that he could not be

---

[1] At first this rescued child was thought to be the daughter of Cynthia Ann Parker, who was still with the Comanches at the time. After a diligent, vain search for the family of the little white girl, Sul chose to adopt, rear, and educate her. "Lizzie" Ross was named in honor of his sweetheart, Lizzie Tinsley, to whom he was engaged at the time. When Sul escorted his mother Catherine to Los Angeles in August 1870, Lizzie Ross went with them. While in California, Lizzie met and married a wealthy merchant living near Los Angeles

moved from under a post oak for five days. The heavy slug missed a vital organ, but the pain from the infected wound was so intense that the feverish Sul begged his "nurse," Caddo John, to kill him and end his misery. On the long return trip to Camp Radziminski, both Van Dorn and Ross were carried on litters suspended between two gentle mules. When the pain became too great, the latter was carried on the shoulders of his Indian scouts. The wasted-looking Ross then rode in a horse-drawn ambulance to Fort Belknap, arriving at the Indian agency on October 18, and heading home to Waco a week later.

In his official report on the Wichita Village campaign, Van Dorn commended Sul highly while Commanding General Winfield Scott singled out the expedition sutler, Mr. J. F. Ward, and Captain Ross as "deserving of the highest praise for their gallantry during the action." The young captain's fame as a military leader spread when the *Dallas Herald* printed an extra edition of Van Dorn's campaign report on October 10. While his mother cared for him at Waco, the convalescing Ross received a highly complimentary letter from General Scott, who offered him a direct cavalry commission in the regular army. Since he had no formal military training, the unassuming young hero passed up the offer of a military career and chose to return to Wesleyan for his senior year.

Most likely, the "love bug" also figured into Sul's declining the army commission. He had been smitten by Elizabeth Dorothy Tinsley, an admirer and the daughter of a neighboring planter. He planned to marry this dark-haired, bright-eyed lass some day and was unwilling to subject her to the dreary, lonely existence of an army wife.

After finishing his A.B. degree in June 1859, Ross went home to find the Texas frontier in turmoil. There had been a renewal of Comanche horse-stealing raids in November 1858, followed by a second Van Dorn-agency Indian expedition the following spring. With agitation led by John R. Baylor, angry Texans had become suspicious of all reserve Indians, and the Reservation War led to their forced removal from Texas in the summer of 1859. On March 17, 1860, Governor Sam Houston authorized Col. Middleton T. Johnson of Tarrant County to raise volunteer companies of mounted rangers and to chastise the Indians. Five frontier counties responded, with the Waco detachment of eighty-four privates led by Capt. J. M. Smith and 1st Lt. Sul Ross. When the Waco company departed for Fort Belknap on April 23, their proud ladies presented Sul with a beautiful ribbon banner. Once the five companies organized into a regiment, Smith was elected as lieutenant colonel on May 18. Ross took his place as Ranger captain, although he was bedridden at the time by a bronchitis attack.

Sul's promotion was resented by Baylor's followers, who despised the younger Ross because his father had been agent at the Brazos Reserve. Since Sul had lived with Indians there, many frontiersmen assumed he would be soft on them. When his unit stopped for water after chasing a raiding party to the Trinity River, a crusty pioneer woman expressed the wish that the Indians would scalp all of his Waco company.

While old Colonel Johnson was away in Galveston taking a new bride, his regiment remained at old Camp Radziminski throughout the summer. Amid a barrage of criticism from frontiersmen, Johnson's regiment was finally disbanded on August 26, 1860. Writing in the *White Man* at Weatherford on September 13, Baylor discribed this Ranger unit as "perfectly harmless" and as the "most *stupendous sell* ever practiced on a frontier people." No wonder a less-than-proud Ross never mentioned his service in this first Ranger company again.

The Battle of Pease River, however, would soon redeem and win everlasting fame for Sul. After visiting the family ranch in Young County, he was in Waco on September 7, 1860. Four days later the surprised — and pleased — Ranger captain was authorized by Governor

Houston to raise a company of sixty mounted volunteers for new service against raiding Indians. After raising his company in Waco, Sul's men reached Fort Belknap on October 17. Almost immediately he received a resolution of no-confidence signed by eighty pro-Baylor residents of Palo Pinto County, who asked this friend of reserve Indians to resign his captaincy and leave the frontier. In the weeks that followed, the embattled leader spent much of the time at his desk preparing accounts and vouchers and badgering Governor Houston for promised supplies.

In late November 1860, war chief Peta Nacona led a series of Comanche raids through Jack, Wise, Parker, and Palo Pinto counties, burning houses, stealing horses, murdering, looting, and raping. On December 2, Capt. J. H. (Jack) Cureton organized a "citizens company" from these counties to pursue Nacona. At the time of the raids, Ross and thirty-two men were out scouting and returned to find that a local posse had tracked the Indians to a winter village on the Pease River. Sul then made plans to "carry the war" to the Comanches. Since he could spare only forty of his Rangers, he asked for help from Capt. Nathan G. Evans, the U.S. commander at Camp Cooper, who detailed 1st Sgt. John W. Spangler and twenty troopers from Company H of the Second Cavalry, to the Ross expedition. In early December, Cureton and his sixty-eight citizens joined forces with the Rangers and cavalrymen. Although Jack was a much older man, Governor Houston's special orders gave Sul supreme command of the combined force.

On December 12, 1860, Ross and Spangler formed an advance party and rode out from Fort Belknap with Cureton's men bringing up the rear. This "right tight" little army was guided northwest by John Socie (or Stuart), a buffalo hunter who knew the Pease River country well. Due to a combination of snow, sleet, bad water, and poor grass, Cureton's men — who were not as well mounted — found it hard to keep up and fell four miles behind. Late in the afternoon on December 18, two of Sul's scouts found signs of the Comanches. Ordering Jack to follow the next day, Ross immediately broke camp and reached Mule Creek, a tributary of the Pease River, at daybreak.

Hidden by the dust clouds of a fresh norther, he scouted ahead to the rise of a rough hill, where he observed a detached Comanche hunting camp some 200 yards away on the creek banks. The squaws were breaking camp and packing and loading buffalo meat for the winter supply. Sul quickly devised plans for a surprise attack: while his Rangers were charging down the ridge with guns blazing, the army troopers would circle around and cut off any retreat.

In the initial attack, some Comanche warriors riding west turned back to fight, hoping to hold back Ross's men until the women and children could escape. After dismounting and putting their horses in a circle as breastworks, the braves soon broke for their mounts and scattered before the withering gunfire. Those who fled toward the sandhills were met head on by the army cavalry.

During the running battle, Sul and Lt. Thomas Kelliher gave chase to an Indian trio, two of them riding double. Kelliher pursued the single rider for two miles before this "damned squaw" (as he called her) reigned up and held a two-year-old baby girl above her. After ordering the lieutenant to look after her (the Indian woman was actually Cynthia Ann Parker), Ross continued to chase the Indians riding double. The larger one was dressed in a chief's regalia and the other, riding behind, was hidden by a buffalo robe. When Sul killed the rear rider, a teenage girl, with his first shot, her dead weight also pulled the warrior off his horse. One of the Indian's arrows hit Ross's mount, and it started to buck wildly. While he was clinging to the pommel of his saddle with one hand, a random shot from Sul's pistol shattered the brave's right arm at the elbow, leaving him with a useless bow.

Once his horse calmed down, Ross shot the "chief" twice more through the body. The Indian struggled to a mesquite sapling and started chanting a wild, weird death song. Just then, Sul's Mexican servant and interpreter, Anton Martinez, rode up and identified the warrior as Chief Peta Nacona. Martinez, a former Comanche captive who knew their language, was instructed to offer surrender. When the defiant brave answered by thrusting at Ross with his lance, Anton begged for permission to shoot him. Although the Ranger captain admired the Indian's bravery, he evidently preferred death to life. Sul gave a reluctant nod of approval for Martinez to "end his misery by a charge of buckshot." Assuming that he had in fact killed Chief Nacona, Ross sent the dead man's accoutrements to Governor Houston to be deposited in the state archives.[2]

Lieutenant Kelliher soon rode up with his Indian captive, an old squaw carrying a small child. She had hard, coarse facial lines and was "very dirty and far from attractive," but Captain Ross noticed that she had blue eyes. Comanche eyes were black and glittery. He had captured a white woman. That night the crying woman told scout

---

[2] For years Peta Nacona's eldest son, Quanah Parker, forbade his people to tell the truth about the man killed by Sul Ross, out of respect to his family. Quanah did not want it denied that General Ross had killed Nacona; if the incident brought any credit to Sul, let the people believe his story. There is a plausible explanation for Parker's attitude: he felt indebted to Ross. In 1874 Quanah advertised in the *Fort Worth Gazette* for a picture of his long-lost mother, Cynthia Ann Parker. Sul, who was then living in Waco, forwarded him a copy of a daguerreotype of her taken by A. F. Corning at Fort Worth in 1862. Only after the death of Ross did Chief Parker choose to set the record straight about the death of his father, Peta Nacona. During a feature speech at the Texas State Fair at Dallas in 1910, Quanah noted:

The history books say General Ross kill my father. This damn lie . . . He not there. After the fight at Mule Creek [junction with Pease River] — two, three, maybe four years — my father sick. I see him die. I want to get that in Texas history — straight up.

Quanah's daughter, Mrs. Neda Parker Birdsong, later identified the victim of Ross as being a Mexican captive named "Nokoni's Joe," a servant of Peta Nacona. According to Mrs. Birdsong, this Mexican slave was Cynthia Ann's personal servant and had stayed near to try and protect her during the Battle of Pease River.

Martinez that she was Chief Nacona's wife, and that she feared for the lives of her two boys, Quanah and Pecos. Mother and daughter were taken to Camp Cooper, where they were attended by Mrs. Evans, wife of the commandant. Thinking that she might be the white girl carried off in the Fort Parker massacre of May 1836, Sul sent word to have Col. Isaac Parker come and try to identify her. At first her uncle's questions brought only a blank stare and Parker finally said, "Maybe we are wrong — poor Cynthia Ann." Upon hearing those words she pressed her hand over her heart, broke into tears, and said, "Cynthia — me Cynthia." After living a quarter of a century with the Comanches, Cynthia Ann Parker was taken to an unhappy reunion with her original family. She tragically returned to "civilization," a melancholy existence, and a premature death. Quanah Parker, the half-breed boy who was taken from his mother, was destined to be the last recognized chief of the Comanches and the richest Indian in the United States when he died.

Although the Battle of Pease River won enduring fame for Sul Ross and helped make him governor of Texas, the surprise attack was really a massacre of unarmed women and Mexican slaves; only one man was killed, with the other thirteen Comanche victims being women. Sul's men suffered no casualties, not even a minor wound. Jack Cureton's men arrived after the fighting and later criticized Ross's men for pushing ahead and keeping all forty-five captured Comanche horses for their own use. After finding a nine-year-old Indian boy hiding in the camp grass, Sul tenderly took the lad up on his horse and later carried him back to Waco. "Pease" Ross was adopted, reared, and educated by the Ranger leader and spent the rest of his life as a citizen of McLennan County.

A pleased Governor Houston met Sul at Waco and offered the following tribute: "Your success in protecting the frontier gives me great satisfaction. I am satisfied that with the same opportunities you would rival if not excel the greatest exploits of McCulloch or Jack Hays." The governor verbally requested that Ross recruit another Ranger company, but written orders to that effect never followed.

Sul was back at Ranger field headquarters on Elm Creek when a special convention met in Austin and passed an ordinance of secession in late January 1861. This ordinance was overwhelmingly approved by the voters on February 23, and took effect on March 2, 1861. During these crisis times, Ross returned to Waco and resigned from the Rangers with "regret and appreciation" on February 12. Governor Houston returned the letter of resignation, asked him to reconsider, and appointed him aide-de-camp with the rank of colonel. When Houston was deposed as governor for refusing to take an oath of allegiance to the Confederate States of America, the new governor, Edward Clark, persuaded Sul to continue Ranger service by protecting the western frontier. After three months of such duty, Ross returned to Waco, where he enlisted as a private in the Confederate cavalry company of his brother Peter. Once the State of Texas declared itself in the Confederacy on March 5, 1861, supporting the South in the Civil War became "the path of duty" for Sul Ross.

During his brief return to civilian life that spring, Sul was involved in the final courtship of his longtime sweetheart, Lizzie Tinsley. Her father, David Augustus Tinsley, was a wealthy cotton planter and physician who had moved to Waco from Macon, Georgia, when Elizabeth was eight. Dr. Tinsley built a white-pillared, front-galleried mansion on acreage adjacent to the Ross farm, where Lizzie blossomed into a charming, vivacious Southern belle with blue eyes, brunette hair, and a fair complexion. Miss Tinsley married Sul Ross in her father's Waco mansion on May 28, 1861, with Methodist minister U.C. Spencer officiating.

Cutting short their honeymoon, Sul left his new bride with her parents on June 3 and departed for Indian

Territory. Governor Clark had commissioned him to make a peace treaty with the remnant reservation tribes near Fort Cobb, seeking either their "active cooperation or friendly inactivity" during the Civil War. When the new groom arrived at the Washita Agency, he found that Confederate commissioners had already signed such a treaty with the remnant tribes on May 15, 1861.

In mid-August, Peter Ross and his Waco cavalry company responded to the call of Confederate Col. B. Warren Stone of Dallas, who was raising a cavalry regiment to fight with Gen. Ben McCulloch in Missouri. Stone's regiment (later designated the Sixth Texas Cavalry) included ten companies totaling 1,150 men from eleven counties; Company G was from Waco. On September 13, Pvt. Sul Ross was elected regimental major by a 3-to-1 margin. Soon after the regiment marched out of Dallas, he was "surprised and mortified" to find Colonel Stone drunk with his men and thus unable to command their respect or obedience. By the time the regiment reached McCulloch's headquarters at Maysville, Arkansas, in mid-October, Stone's men were short on food and ammunition.

General McCulloch wanted to carry the war to the Jayhawkers (antislavery guerrillas) in Kansas but was forced to divert a cavalry force, including Stone's regiment, to Carthage, Missouri. There they bolstered retreating Confederate General Sterling Price, who was being chased by Gen. John C. Fremont. Twice in early November, McCulloch sent Ross to scout the Union army near Springfield then led by Gen. David Hunter, who soon retreated to St. Louis. As a result, McCulloch ordered his men back to winter quarters on the Arkansas River, where Sul took a sixty-day leave of absence before rejoining his regiment in early 1862.

After 12,000 Union troops under Gen. Samuel R. Curtis advanced to a rise called Pea Ridge in northwest Arkansas on February 18, 1862, Price and McCulloch again joined forces near Elkhorn Tavern in the Boston Mountains. Seeing that the Federal supply lines were overextended, McCulloch sent Ross and 500 cavalry troops on a raid seventy miles behind enemy lines. Skirting to the east of Curtis's army, Sul's men attacked Keetsville, Missouri, and destroyed a Union supply train. This daring assault was highly praised by Colonel Stone and enhanced Ross's growing reputation as a scout and raider.

On March 3, 1862, Maj. Gen. Earl Van Dorn assumed command of McCulloch's and Price's combined force of 16,000 troops. He immediately decided to make a forced march to Curtis's Union camp on Sugar Creek, then attack from the rear using flanking movements rather than risk a frontal assault. As he rode by with Stone's regiment, Sul saw that Van Dorn's exhausted, overmarched infantry were lying by the roadside "overcome with hunger and fatigue." When the Battle of Pea Ridge began at dawn on March 7, the flanking movement proved to be too slow; Price and McCulloch's men were still five miles apart and thus fighting on two fronts. After the battle was lost and Ben McCulloch was killed, Ross placed the blame on Van Dorn for overmarching and underfeeding his troops and for not coordinating his plan of attack.

After retreating deep into Arkansas, Van Dorn was ordered to cross the Mississippi and help Gen. Albert Sidney Johnston later that month. In early April 1862, the cavalry regiments were sent to Des Arc, Arkansas, dismounted, and the horses sent back to Texas. This "breach of faith" put the Sixth Texas Cavalry on foot, and the regiment was sent to Memphis, Tennessee, by steamboat. While camped there, the Texans learned that the Confederate Conscription Act of April 16, 1862, had given all troops under arms a three-year extension of duty. When the ambitious Colonel Stone traveled to Richmond, Virginia, seeking promotion to brigadier general under terms of the act, the men of the Sixth announced they would elect Ross to regimental command even over his protest. After the Sixth was detailed from Van Dorn's army and ordered to reinforce the army of Gen. P. G. T. Beauregard at Corinth, Mississippi, they traveled there by rail on twenty flatcars pulled by one locomotive of the Memphis and Charleston Railroad. Once the Texans reached Corinth, they elected Sul as regimental colonel on May 8, 1862.

In an eight-week period, Ross's weight fell to 125 pounds as he fought a lingering cold and fever. During that trying summer, Colonel Ross drilled his barefooted men — half of whom were sick with measles, mumps, or malaria — in infantry tactics. Their frustrated leader also wrote a "very saucy note" to his superiors, which resulted in a new supply of clothing. By the end of summer, the Sixth was chosen to be remounted by Confederate leaders, who expected "something brilliant" from Ross's men.

In mid-September 1862, General Price and 17,000 troops were ordered to keep Union forces in Mississippi from reinforcing Gen. Don Carlos Buell in central Tennessee. During the march north the still-on-foot Texans made quite an impression on their division commander, West Pointer Dabney H. Maury, who described the Sixth as "one of the finest bodies of men ever seen in any service," and their colonel as being "a very handsome, poetical-looking young fellow with voice and manner gentle as a woman's, and the heart of a true soldier of Texas." Poor health and bouts of homesickness left Sul in a depressed state of mind, but he found that drilling his troops for long hours in the hot sun seemed to lift his spirits.

On September 14, Price's army entered Iuka, Mississippi, a fashionable town on the Memphis and Charleston Railroad line, where they fought a stalemated battle with five retreating Union divisions. Soon thereafter, Van Dorn reassumed command of Price's forces and was assigned 22,000 Confederate troops for the purpose of taking Corinth, a key rail and highway center, from Gen. William S. Rosecrans and 15,000 Federal forces.

Van Dorn's army attacked early in the morning on October 3 and drove the Yankees back from their earthworks to a second line of defense, a battery of nine guns on a hill. With Ross in the lead, his dismounted Texas cavalry gave a loud shout for Texas, made a "fearful" charge, and captured the battery in spite of heavy losses. By this time the Sixth was a half-mile in front of the Confederate lines and facing heavy siege guns, the final Union line of defense. Still awaiting reinforcements and fearing that his men would be flanked, Sul chose to withdraw from such an exposed position.

The next day at sunup, the Sixth Cavalry was involved in a frontal assault on the Robinett battery. During a furious charge across a 300-yard-wide belt of fallen trees, Ross was thrown from his white mare, starting the false rumor that he had been killed. After reaching the Federal breastworks, the Sixth captured the eastern edge of Robinett just long enough to hoist the Confederate flag. Union reinforcements soon forced a withdrawal, which ended the final Confederate attempt to take Corinth. On October 5, Colonel Ross confronted an enemy force ten times his rearguard of 700 riflemen, ten miles northwest of town. His heroic leadership in repulsing three assaults by 6,500 Union troops at the Hatchie River bridge led Dabney Maury to report that Sul was the most distinguished officer during the Corinth campaign. The event brought him a promotion to brigadier general.

Several weeks later, the Sixth's horses finally arrived, and the regiment was transferred to the cavalry brigade of Col. William H. "Red" Jackson, a West Pointer from Tennessee. In early November, Sul was furloughed to Texas to take his wounded brother home. He was back to duty, but more homesick than ever, by mid-January 1863; en route, he wrote Lizzie two loving letters in which he confessed, "The call of duty alone prompted me to leave you when my heart and all my feelings rebelled against it." He returned to find Van Dorn as chief of the cavalry corps in the West and moving into Tennessee. The Texas Cavalry Brigade was now under the nominal command of Col. John W. Whitfield, a rheumatic veteran of the Mexican War who was twenty years older than Sul. The frustrated Ross was soon complaining that Whitfield "frolicked" around, leaving him with all the actual work to do.

On April 10, 1863, Van Dorn's corps fought in the Battle of Franklin, but the dismounted Texans were held in reserve. When Artillery Captain S. L. Freeman was murdered after surrendering, the war became even more brutal in nature. After the battle, Van Dorn's cavalry corps held a review at Spring Hill, where a reporter for the *Mobile Register and Advertiser* described the Texas Brigade as follows:

> Here come those rollicking, rascally, brave Texans; and there at their head is a young man apparently twenty-eight years of age, with wavy black hair, black moustache, an olive complexion, fine expressive features, and graceful form. This is Colonel Ross, of the Sixth Texas . . .
>
> What singular looking customers those Texans are, with their large brimmed hats, dark features, shaggy Mexican mustangs, and a lariet [*sic*] . . . around the pummel of their saddles. They are said to be unmerciful to prisoners, but are a tower of strength when there is a fight on hand.

On May 7, 1863, Van Dorn was killed by an angry husband whose wife he had seduced. Red Jackson's division was then assigned to Joseph E. Johnston's army and the defense of Vicksburg. Although John Whitfield had been promoted to brigadier general, Jackson considered him "entirely unfit for cavalry" and wanted Ross to command the brigade. After Vicksburg fell on July 4, 1863, the Texas Brigade was ordered into central Mississippi, then sent on raids into Tennessee.

In late November, Sul received sad news from home: his and Lizzie's first baby had died. At Moscow, Tennessee, on December 3, Ross's brigade trounced Col. Edward Hatch's Federal cavalry as they were crossing the Wolf

River bridge; some of the panic-stricken Yankees sought to escape by jumping their horses off the bridge.

From September 1863 until April 1864, recurring tertian malaria brought Sul attacks of fever and chills every third day. The cold that settled in his lungs resulted in chronic bronchitis. It was during this period that the grumbling of Texans about the inept leadership of feeble, old General Whitfield came to the attention of Robert E. Lee. Knowing that the men loved and respected the popular Ross, Lee solved the problem by promoting Sul to brigadier general and giving him brigade command in late January 1864. Reaction was immediate. On February 1, the Third Texas Cavalry reenlisted to a man. The modest Sul even expressed the fear that most of his men would desert if he was killed, and admitted that his authority was based on "their love for me as an individual."

General Ross's Texas Brigade was sent to Rome, Georgia, in April 1864, where they joined General Johnston in his retreat before Sherman's march to the south. The Texans first met the enemy in force on May 17, the beginning of eighty-six skirmishes fought during a 100-day period under fire and without real rest. Sul had one close brush with death when fired on by Federal troops after tarrying on the front lines to read letters from home. Fighting associated with the fall of Atlanta continued until September 3.

A worn-out Ross later admitted that the strain of "fighting all the time" for eighteen months had aged him ten years. His brigade suffered twenty-five percent losses during the Atlanta campaign, with available manpower dropping from 1,000 to barely 700 men. While his men were on picket duty near Macon, Georgia, that September, Sul asked former Texas governor Francis Lubbock, who was passing through en route to Richmond, for his assistance in obtaining a brigade-wide furlough. In his view even a transfer to Mississippi and the prospect of individual leaves might prevent a mass desertion by the brigade.

Ross was to put forth a noble effort in his final active operation, the disastrous Tennessee campaign of November-December 1864. After being assigned to Gen. John Bell Hood, the Texans led the Confederate advance into Tennessee, but some deserted after Hood's demoralizing defeat at Nashville in mid-December. Sul's men were the last cavalry unit in a rear guard trying to protect the Confederate army fleeing south. After being attacked for two weeks by pursuing Union forces, the chase finally stopped when the Texans crossed the Tennessee River on December 27. In his official report of the campaign, General Ross said he suffered twelve killed and seventy wounded but captured 550 prisoners along with enough overcoats and blankets for his whole command. While reporting from Corinth in January 1865, Sul was too sick to leave his room for three days, and his letter to Lizzie resembled the handwriting of an old man.

In late January, Ross's brigade was assigned to picket duty at Vicksburg. General Hood had requested a brigade furlough, but the Confederate secretary of war recommended leaves of only twenty days, prompting 180 of the Texans to desert with no attempt to stop them. Once a furlough for half of the brigade came through in mid-February, their exhausted, sickly leader left for Texas on a ninety-day leave of absence on March 13; this was the last time that Sul Ross saw his troops. Lee had surrendered the Army of Northern Virginia by the time Sul experienced a joyous family reunion at Waco. He was not present when the Texas regiments lay down their arms at Jackson, Mississippi, on May 13, 1865. According to the *Dallas Herald,* Ross's Texas Brigade had 4,700 men when it crossed the Mississippi River in May 1862; three years and 235 engagements later, only 600 remained. Amazingly, Sul participated in 135 engagements with the enemy and had five horses shot out from under him, yet suffered no serious wounds during the Civil War.

He returned to Waco a feeble, impoverished hero,

and little is known of Ross until he returned to public life in 1873. Since he was above the rank of colonel, the ex-Confederate had to apply for special pardon for his treason against the United States; he did so in Austin on August 4, 1865, but his presidential pardon did not come until two years later.

At war's end the twenty-six-year-old Ross had only land with which to make a living. He owned a 5.41-acre tract in Waco, along with 160 acres of rich bottomland on the South Bosque River west of town. Since farming and hunting were in his blood, he readily built a farm cabin where he and Lizzie had their second child, Mervin, on January 2, 1866. After the Radical Republicans gained control of the U.S. Congress, they pushed through their own vindictive Reconstruction plan, which again disqualified Sul from voting or even serving as a juror.

During this period of turmoil, he chose to shun politics while quietly prospering as a farmer and landowner. By drawing on family financial resources, he was able to purchase about 1,000 acres of farmland by the end of the decade. As Waco became a cotton, wheat, and beef center after the war, Sul branched out in the cattle business. He and brother Pete made several trail drives to New Orleans, and the younger Ross was raising and breeding pedigreed Durham (Shorthorn) cattle by the mid-1870s. His farming and cattle ventures enabled Sul to send his children to private schools and to build a fine family home on Austin Avenue in Waco.

The Ross family did have one close call, however, during the Reconstruction period. While Waco was under Union military occupation in 1868, local legend has it that Shapley Ross assaulted a Union soldier, was arrested, but managed to escape by flashing the secret Masonic distress signal. He wisely chose to travel to southern California "for his health," where Shapley was joined by his oldest son Peter. In August 1870, Sul escorted his mother Catherine and his sister Lizzie (the white girl rescued from the Comanches) from Waco to Los Angeles for a family reunion. A few weeks later, his sons persuaded the senior Ross that he could safely return home.

Starting in 1868, Longhorn herds bound for Dodge City, Kansas, passed through Waco, bringing the lawlessness associated with a trail town. The railroad arrived at Waco in 1871 and brought a string of saloons, gambling halls, and bawdy houses. This town of 5,000 soon developed a reputation as a "Six-shooter Depot," where killings were commonplace. The problem was compounded by a 48,708-acre wilderness directly across the shallow Brazos from Waco. This eleven-square-league Tomás de la Vega grant had been in litigation for twenty-two years and had become a no-man's land affording a hideout for criminals, rustlers, and horse and timber thieves (or "choppers"). Peaceful townspeople called these desperadoes "Modocs," who brazenly led jailbreaks, shot up the town, and occupied the Bridge Street saloon from time to time.

Desperate friends and fellow citizens urged Sul Ross in 1873 to run for sheriff of McLennan County. He was elected to the post without campaigning and took office in January 1874, with brother Peter as his deputy. Their first priority was cleaning out the de la Vega grant; in less than two years, the two arrested over 700 outlaws there. By August 1874, the *Waco Daily Examiner* was proudly warning thieves that their sheriff was a "dead shot" who did not miss his mark.

That November a new county jail was completed, a facility guaranteed to hold its prisoners. The most noteworthy arrest Sheriff Ross made was that of Belle Star, the "Bandit Queen." After running a Dallas livery stable as a cover for horse stealing, Belle and a new boyfriend named McManus went to the Waco area after 1875. Armed with a Dallas telegraphic warrant for her arrest, Sul nabbed Belle en route to her Cook Creek farm, then returned her to Dallas to face charges.

It was Ross who originated the Sheriff's Association of Texas in 1874 for the purpose of "more successfully aiding each other as officers." When sixty-five county sheriffs held their first meeting at Corsicana that August, Sul called the gathering to order. After being elected as the Waco delegate to the Constitutional Convention of 1875, he resigned as county sheriff in August and was succeeded by brother Peter. By then his jurisdiction had a statewide reputation for law and order, and Sul was known as the "Model Sheriff of Texas."

When ninety delegates met in Austin on September 6, 1875, their foremost objective was to rid the state of the 1869 Republican constitution forced on Texas by Reconstruction. Among the familiar faces Ross saw there were two old comrades-in-arms, "Rip" Ford and John W. Whitfield. Sul was among the forty-one farmers represented, while twenty-eight delegates were lawyers.

Much of his input was in committee, where he spoke for the minority in several losing causes. For example, he sought unsuccessfully to have all land taxed in the county where it was located. At the time, thirty-five million acres of Texas land was owned by absentee nonresident landlords, who thus continued to escape taxation. When Ross proposed that the nine million acres of earlier land grants, forfeited by railroads failing to complete service, should be assigned to the permanent school fund, he again met defeat. A coalition of Grangers and Republicans stymied Sul's efforts to require a poll tax as a prerequisite for voting in Texas. In one rare instance, he took to the floor to deliver a lengthy speech against "illiberally" cutting the salaries of district and supreme court judges to the point of being unable to support their families. To Ross, such a salary reduction was a sure way *not* to attract men of intelligence and high character to the Texas bench. This plea also went unheeded, but he did help insure that Texas cities would be protected from unfair railroad rates.

Sul missed only five of the sixty-eight days the convention was in session and even managed to find time for some drill-team judging. When the constitutional convention completed its work on November 24, 1875, he was among the twelve delegates appointed to draft an address to the people of Texas explaining the principles and reforms of the new constitution.

At this time Ross had no further political ambitions and was more than happy to return to family and farm. He remained out of public view until the summer of 1878, when one of his ex-cavalrymen, Victor M. Rose, editor of the *Victoria Advocate,* published a letter detailing Sul's suitability for high office. Rose intended to write a history of his Confederate brigade, and its leader endorsed the "commendable" project, promising financial support and whatever information his faulty memory could provide.

In the spring of 1880, Victor led an unsuccessful effort to draft Ross for the gubernatorial race. When the two leading contenders for the Texas Senate deadlocked the nominating convention that fall, Sul consented to run as a compromise candidate from the Twenty-second District. Rose wrote a biographical sketch guaranteed to "swell his vote greatly," and Ross won an easy victory on the Democratic ticket.

Soon after the balding, forty-two-year-old Confederate hero took his seat in the Seventeenth Legislature, news came that his month-old son was dead. He rushed back to Waco and spent a week with Lizzie, whose health was broken by the deaths of the baby and her mother.

In the first legislative session of 1881, Senator Ross introduced a petition of McLennan County citizens that resulted in putting a prohibition amendment on the ballot in the upcoming September elections. In the second session this fiscal conservative was appointed chairman of the Committee on Finance. After a fire destroyed the old Capitol in early November 1881, a special session of the legislature met in April 1882 to provide for temporary housing of state offices. Just before that session ended, the Senate passed a reapportionment bill which reduced Ross's four-year term to two years, and he declined to run for another term.

Since 1878, Sul had been under pressure to run for governor. His stated reluctance arose from the "questionable methods" used to gain that office. His most persistent champion, editor Victor Rose, renewed his campaign on February 26, 1884. In a letter to the influential *Galveston Daily News,* Victor praised Ross for his honesty, competence, and probity. The very next day, a wavering Sul wrote Rose to outline the impossibility of his candidacy; as he saw it, those times of frontier tensions between farmer and rancher demanded bold actions and words, not mere personal glory. By late 1885, however, Ross had decided to make the race, with the *Waco Daily Examiner* as his strongest, most vocal supporter.

On February 25, 1886, Sul announced his candidacy for governor in an interview with the *Galveston Daily News,* which credited him with giving "frank, manly, concise and straightforward" views on the main issues. On the question of public school lands, he favored their sale to actual settlers at low interest rates rather than leases of these lands by the State Land Board; he opposed statewide prohibition, seeing no need to change local option laws then in effect; the public must be protected from railroad combinations and arbitrary actions until competition solved the problem; with regard to the Knights of Labor and the Farmers' Alliance, he admitted little knowledge of their aims but did deplore their lawless means.

Sul's most formidable Democratic opponent was State Comptroller William J. Swain, who was endorsed by most of the large daily papers. Swain came under attack, however, for nepotism, putting phony names on the state payroll, the treasury deficit, and his plan to substitute Indiana limestone for Texas granite in building the new Capitol. Ross spent May and June campaigning in north and central Texas, but spent no money beyond his travel expenses. Twice he considered withdrawing from the race, according to his campaign manager, George Clark. Those political enemies who resented his "poaching" on their turf referred to Sul as the "little cavalryman" and the "war horse." He received great support, however, from Texas Confederate veterans and non-Alliance farmers and was endorsed by numerous county conventions in July.

On August 10, 1886, the Democratic state convention met in a Galveston skating rink. On the second day, Ross made a rather lackluster twenty-five-minute speech described as a disappointment to his friends. During the convention the *Galveston News* noted:

> General Ross is a good-looking man . . . He stands straight as an arrow and is not far from six feet high . . . his general appearance did not denote perfect health. General Ross is no orator. He is not even an ordinarily good speaker. He has a camp meeting drawl and the intonations of his voice sound unpleasant.

After leading Swain on the first ballot by a 433–99 margin, all of Sul's opponents withdrew; he was nominated by acclamation and carried into the convention hall on his supporters' shoulders. A *Galveston News* reporter surmised that fear of the general's popularity led the opportunistic political machine to support Ross and thus maintain their position. Perhaps his proud mother best summed up the public mood when she proclaimed, "Sul will do right wherever they put him."

On what the *Waco Daily Examiner* described as "The Grandest Day" in city history, he was welcomed home by Lizzie, their six surviving children, and townspeople who treated him like a conquering hero. When the general election was held on November 2, he won an overwhelming victory with 228,776 votes, compared to 65,236 for the Republican candidate and 19,186 for the Prohibitionist.

On Inauguration Day, January 19, 1887, Governor Ross gave a detailed, hour-long address followed that evening by an elaborate inauguration ball and dinner in the new Driskill Hotel, starting a longtime tradition. On orders of the new "First Family," no intoxicating beverages were served to the thousand guests attending the

sumptuous affair. There was a problem with one prominent "gate-crasher," seventy-six-year-old Shapley Ross,
who had busied himself making the rounds of the Austin
bars during the day. When the tipsy father of the governor arrived at the inauguration ball, a doorkeeper stiffly
demanded to see his invitation. Old Shapley responded
by roaring out a series of profanities and shouting, "If I
don't get in there, I'll call my boy, Sul, and we'll take this
place apart!" Not surprisingly, he got in.

During Ross's first of two rather quiet terms, there
were improvements in the system of selling and leasing
public lands, and a new capitol was completed. The land
reforms included classifying public lands so as to know
their value and insure title and accurate boundaries,
selling acreage at low interest over a long period of time,
controlling public lands through a single authority (the
Commissioner of the Land Office), and legislation pun-
ishing those who occupied and used state lands illegally.
As a result of these reforms, some 3.5 million acres of
school, university, and asylum land were sold. By 1890,
the land commissioner could proudly take note of the unprecedented number of new counties being organized.

The cornerstone of the new capitol was laid on March
2, 1885. As an ex officio member of the Capitol Board,
Governor Ross saw to the safe construction of the capitol
dome. The new red granite capitol was completed on May
8, 1888, and a five-day dedication celebration was held a
week later. A crowd of 9,000, including three former governors and General Mexia of Mexico, watched a beaming
Ross deliver an "eloquent and feeling address." The main
dedicatory speaker was Temple Houston, the Panhan-
dle's new state senator. Temple was the youngest of Sam
and Margaret Lea Houston's eight children and the first
child born in the present Governor's Mansion at Austin.

There were two other noteworthy developments in
Sul's first term. When the Twentieth Legislature passed
a prohibition constitutional amendment, the governor
drafted a vigorous letter condemning this governmental

effort at "changing the moral convictions of its subjects by force," and the proposed amendment was soundly rejected by the voters in August 1887. Ross also enjoyed the distinction of being the first and only governor ever to call a special legislative session (April-May 1888) to deal with a treasury surplus. Rather than cut the ad valorem tax rate, he proposed to remit one-third of the state surplus to the taxpayer; the balance would be spent on such projects as furnishing the new capitol, erecting a memorial to Texas veterans, increasing asylum space, and raising the salary of public school teachers. The legislature followed his suggestions on spending the surplus but ignored the governor by choosing to cut the tax rate.

In the election of 1888, Ross ran unopposed within the Democratic party, and the Republicans ran no candidate against him in the fall. His only serious opponent, Marion Martin, was supported by a coalition of Prohibitionists, Knights of Labor, and radical farmers, but Sul defeated Martin by 151,891 votes. The two major challenges of his second term came about as a result of lawlessness. One of these problems had been festering since 1877, when a young salesman, John W. "Bet-a-Million" Gates, arrived at San Antonio and sold Texas cattlemen on the idea of fencing their ranges with barbed wire. By 1883, practically all the cattle country of south and central Texas had been fenced. That year, fence-cutting occurred in more than half of the 171 counties of the state. To deal with this crisis, Governor Ireland called a special session of the legislature, which passed laws making fence-cutting a felony early in 1884.

In mid-1888, there was a new rash of fence-cutting, particularly in those areas where the farm met the frontier. That summer, miles of wire were cut on some of the largest ranches in Navarro County. When Sheriff West asked for state help, Governor Ross sent two Rangers, Sgt. Ira Aten and "Fiddling Jim" King, to investigate and make arrests. By early fall, all of the fences west of the Houston & Texas Central Railway were down in the county. At this point the frustrated Sergeant Aten came up with a lethal solution: placing small bombs (dynamite stuffed into concealed shotgun barrels) at intervals along new and intact fences in the county. The booby trap would explode only if set off by tampering with the attached wire. Once one was set off, fear would put a stop to the illegal practice; as Ira put it, "When one of my bombs explodes, all fence cutters will hear of it most likely."

After making a written proposal for deploying such "dynamite bombs" to Capt. L. P. Sieker on October 15, 1888, Aten was ordered *not* to do so and to report to Sieker at Austin. The Ranger sergeant disobeyed the order and took a train to Dallas, where he purchased fifty pounds of dynamite and twenty-four dynamite caps. Only after planting all the bombs in the Richland vicinity, and telling ranchers how to use them, did Aten report to Austin. According to Ira, Sieker "frowned" on the scheme and sent him to see Governor Ross, who angrily dressed him down after hearing the story. Aten later recalled that Sul's bald head got "redder and redder" during the meeting, and that he expected to be "court-martialed and then shot." A compromise was finally reached whereby the Ranger would return to Navarro County and remove the bombs. Instead, Aten exploded the bombs on the Love brothers' ranch as a crowd from all over the county watched. This demonstration brought an abrupt end to the Navarro County Fence War, and Ira was not fired. Evidently, the pragmatic Ross appreciated a fellow Ranger who could get results.

The governor used the force of his popularity and prestige to personally intervene in bringing an end to the Jaybird-Woodpecker War, an outbreak of mob lawlessness in Fort Bend County. No county had been more fiercely secessionist, and ninety percent of its white males performed Confederate military service. During Reconstruction, enfranchised former slaves allied with a small group of whites (later called the "Woodpeckers") and gained political ascendancy in the county. Even after the state Reconstruction government collapsed, the native white supremacist Democrats could not dislodge them for a decade. Organized opposition to the hated "courthouse gang" came with the formation of the Young Men's Democratic Club of Richmond (or "Jaybirds") in 1885. The bitter struggle led to violence on August 2, 1888, when a local Negro, William Caldwell, murdered his employer, J. M. Shamblin, leader of the Young Democrats and plantation owner who had sought to control the vote of his Negroes. The situation got out of hand after other black suspects were run out of the county by a Jaybird mob, and blacks vowed to make an armed stand rather than flee. When County Sheriff Jim Garvey — the self-proclaimed "King of the Woodpeckers" — telegraphed the governor's office for help, Ross called out two militia companies to enforce an uneasy peace for four months.

On June 21, 1889, the Woodpecker tax assessor, Kyle Terry, killed lawyer Ned Gibson with blasts from a double-barreled shotgun. Since Ned had two other brothers in Richmond, his murder turned the Jaybird-Woodpecker feud into a personal vendetta. In July, the two factions agreed not to carry Winchesters about town, thus maintaining a sort of truce. However, the Jaybirds stashed their rifles in stores along Morton Street while the Woodpeckers made an arsenal of the courthouse. Upon hearing rumors that "hell might break loose" in Richmond, Governor Ross ordered Adj. Gen. W. H. King to dispatch a Ranger force there. In early August, Capt. Frank Jones, Sgt. Ira Aten, and six privates from Company D pitched camp on the edge of town, then patrolled the streets from dawn to midnight for two weeks. When some forty of the younger Jaybirds left town for a beach party, Captain Jones took three of the Rangers to another assignment.

On the morning of August 16, 1889, the Jaybird beach party rushed back to Richmond. About 6:00 that evening, Judge J. W. Parker — with Winchester in hand — encountered Volney and Guilf Gibson on Morton

Street. Shots were fired, and the badly wounded Parker galloped to the safety of the courthouse. When the shooting began, Sergeant Aten and two Rangers raced toward the courthouse, where they saw Sheriff Garvey and three deputies standing in the yard. In the meantime, twenty-six Jaybirds had grabbed their Winchesters and poured out of the Brahma Bull and Red Hot Bar. Led by Volney Gibson and saloon owner Henry H. "Red Hot" Frost, the armed Jaybirds slowly marched the three blocks down Morton Street to the old courthouse. After the sheriff told him to stay out of the showdown, Sergeant Aten and his Rangers made a fruitless effort to hold back the Jaybird mob before Ira said, "Save yourself, Boys, this isn't our fight." Just then, leaders Garvey and Frost met face-to-face in front of the courthouse and fired at point-blank range; the sheriff fell dead at a hitching post, with seven bullets in him, while Frost was left mortally wounded with a gaping hole in his stomach. The Jaybirds on the open street then opened fire on the outnumbered Woodpeckers hiding in the courthouse. In twenty minutes, several hundred volleys were fired by about thirty-five well-armed men. Amazingly, there were only four dead and an unknown number of wounded in the Battle of Richmond.

As the sun set on bloody Morton Street, Sergeant Aten was sending the following telegram to Governor Ross: "Street fight just occurred between the two factions. Many killed and wounded. Send militia." Sul immediately ordered the Houston Light Guard to Richmond, and a Southern Pacific special train had the company there shortly after midnight. The next morning found Richmond under martial law. On the evening of August 17, Governor Ross arrived by train, along with the Brenham Grays, and went to the National Hotel to take personal charge in the role of mediator. He first called in Sergeant Aten and commended him for his courageous effort to prevent the pitched battle. Ira seemed embarrassed by his failure to stop the mobs until the governor remarked with a chuckle, "Sergeant, you know the old saying about one Ranger being able to handle one mob. But nobody ever demanded that two Rangers be able to stop two mobs."

At noon on Sunday, August 18, Sul met with a Jaybird committee chaired by Clem Bassett, then conferred with a Woodpecker delegation at 3:30 P.M. His message to both factions was blunt and to the point:

> . . . you say that you are law-abiding citizens, but I must tell you that your section is shunned because of its ugly reputation — your section is crushed down; if the present county officers are disposed of by military power that is not democratic . . .

Taking the initiative, Governor Ross then told each group,

> Since there is no sheriff, the commissioners court should appoint one satisfactory to both parties; . . . one who does not live in the county — and, of course, a disinterested party.

After rejecting Clem Bassett, the Jaybird candidate for the position, Sul suggested Ranger Sergeant Aten as an ideal compromise candidate, an outsider who could keep the lid on. On the morning of August 20, the commissioners court approved the twenty-six-year-old Aten as the provisional sheriff of Fort Bend County. Late that evening, Ross and the two militia companies left Richmond; before departing he gave a reporter his assessment of the situation:

> I think that peace is restored permanently. I see the ladies are out in the street again. I noticed a dozen this evening and this is an indication that there is no interest on the part of the citizens to create any further disturbance.

Less than a week after the Richmond gun battle, Ira Aten was the new county sheriff and Governor Ross was back in Austin. The leading Woodpecker families left Fort Bend County within months, and the Jaybirds peacefully regained political control. In her book *The Jay Birds of Fort Bend County,* Pauline Yelderman sums up the role of Sul Ross as follows:

> No doubt Governor Ross, with his wise and conciliatory advice, was largely responsible for restoring peace and quiet to troubled Richmond and Fort Bend County. However, the governor had something else going for him . . . he was a great salesman and never hesitated to use his personal magnetism to persuade others to accept his views.

During his two terms as governor of Texas, Ross brought character, honesty, strength, and dignity to that office. Plain in dress and manner, he was always accessible to the people and was often seen swapping tales and discussing current events with ordinary citizens. Concerned about improving the welfare of others, Sul saw to the construction of a state orphanage, two state mental institutions, and a Confederate home for indigent and disabled Texas veterans. He also persuaded the legislature to purchase 696 acres near Gatesville for the purpose of creating an open farm reformatory for juvenile offenders. It seems that he was ahead of his time in trying to raise public education standards in Texas. Two such progressive recommendations — mandating local taxation to support public schools and requiring the state to provide students with either free or low-cost textbooks — were not enacted by the legislature.

As the 1890 gubernatorial race approached, Ross quickly squashed rumors that he might seek a then unprecedented third term. His lieutenant governor, Thomas B. Wheeler, was opposed by progressive Attorney General James S. Hogg, whose major goal was the creation of a state railroad commission. At the time, many Texans feared that Collis P. Huntington's Southern Pacific was on the verge of gaining total control of state government. To the huge Hogg, the issue in 1890 was simple and clearcut: "Shall the people or the corporations rule Texas?" The more conservative Ross opposed the concept of a regulatory commission, contending that such a "costly and useless luxury" would neither bring relief nor correct railroad abuses. He also faulted the commission concept since it took power from elected representatives and gave it to a powerful appointive body not as responsive to the public. Despite his stated opposition, the Democrats included a commission plank in the party platform, Hogg carried the state in November, and the voters approved a railroad commission amendment.

When Sul Ross left office in January 1891, a final public duty beckoned, saving the faltering Agricultural and Mechanical College of Texas.[3] The school had opened its

---

[3] Texas A&M is a land grant college established under terms of the federal Morrill Act of 1862, which stipulated that such schools teach agriculture and the mechanical arts, and require military training. As the state's first tax-supported college, A&M began classes at College Station on October 4, 1876, after Brazos County donated 2,416 acres for the campus. The first board of directors of Texas A&M met in the summer of 1875 and elected Jefferson Davis as president of the college at an annual salary of $4,000. The former president of the Confederacy wanted to accept the offer, despite the opposition of family and friends who thought his duties would be too arduous. When Davis "finally yielded and declined the presidency with regret," the A&M board appointed his choice, T. S. Gathright, as first president, and the college opened with an enrollment of 107 and six professors. It seems appropriate that the uniform of the A&M cadet corps resembled the official uniform of a Confederate soldier.

There were problems from the beginning. It was difficult to offer agricultural instruction with no books on the subject. Such instruction utilized research carried out in Illinois and Wisconsin, states with soils and climate unlike that of Texas. Farmers thought that teaching agriculture in the classroom was "Yankee silliness." Due to its military character, some parents sent their incorrigible sons to A&M simply for a needed dose of discipline, which may account for an early rule forbidding dueling on campus. To further complicate matters, President Gathright opposed the required military training. Because of chronic dissension on campus, the board finally asked the entire faculty to resign.

In 1879, the new president, James Garland James, hired the staff of Austin's Texas Military Institute as the new A&M faculty. After the University of Texas opened in 1883, it was suggested that A&M

doors in the fall of 1876, but enrolled less than 100 students by 1879. A few years later, the office of president was abolished and the chief executive position was held by the chairman of the A&M faculty. In the late 1880s, this individual was Louis Lowry McInnis, professor of mathematics. The decade did bring internal improvements in teaching, equipment, and research facilities, but the general public remained skeptical of the scientific agriculture being taught there. The college's image was also tarnished by off-campus rumors of student discontent, discipline problems, and faculty squabbles and unrest. This general state of disarray is revealed in a letter by student Lucius Holman. Writing to his mother on October 10, 1888, the pessimistic Holman said,

> Ma, I am sorry to say that this school is going down faster than I ever saw . . . I heard two professors talking about it yesterday. They said in two more years that it would not be worth sending to. They are not managing it rite [*sic*] but I think it will last long enough for me to graduate . . . that is, I hope so.

The state legislature had also lost confidence in Texas A&M. Most lawmakers assumed that increased college appropriations would likely be squandered.

By 1890, the embattled A&M board of directors had reached an overriding consensus: the school *must* have a president independent of the faculty, with such a position being filled by some prominent individual. On July 1, 1890, the board unanimously offered the presidency of A&M to Governor Ross; some members even wanted him to resign and begin this new job at once. News of the offer leaked to the press within a week, prompting the *Galveston Daily News* to editorialize that Sul's "fatherly and pa-

---

should offer *only* agricultural and mechanical courses. Ex-Governor Oran Roberts said it was outrageous that Aggies could take such real university courses as Latin, Greek, French, law, and medicine at state expense. There was even talk of converting the College Station campus into a mental institution.

triotic impulses" and his "firm executive hand" would surely benefit the struggling college.

Several factors weighed against Ross's accepting the A&M presidency: He was eager to retire to a long-neglected farm; going to College Station would involve yet another separation from family and friends in the Waco area; he had two other offers paying more than the yearly A&M salary of $3,500. Also, since most of the board members offering him the job were his own appointees, there was a question of ethics. After much soul-searching, the old soldier finally decided that his future duty lay in College Station, and he formally accepted the presidency on August 8. In a long letter, Ross endorsed the importance of agricultural and military training and expressed his wish that the school become the "pride of the State."

While Sul was serving out his final months as governor, the A&M board of directors "cleaned house" on campus. After abolishing the position of chairman of the faculty, the board chose not to rehire ex-chairman McInnis as a math professor. Others were asked to resign, while many of the faculty and staff chose to leave. With board actions serving to remove factional leaders on both sides, the incoming president would be in a position to hire rather than fire employees. This wholesale personnel turnover did, however, mark the beginning of a bitter college feud.

Once Ross accepted the presidency, there was a drastic change in the public perception of A&M. Those men who had served under the general now wanted to send their sons to school there. The fall session of 1890–91 brought the largest enrollment in ten years. The college had facilities for 250 students; twice that many tried to enroll, and 316 were accepted. Under its new leadership, A&M also enjoyed greater credibility with the legislature. Both a healthy increase in state appropriations and "fine attendance from the best families in the state" were attributed to Sul's influence.

The day after Jim Hogg's inauguration ball in Austin, Ross and his family arrived at College Station. The new president formally took charge on February 2, 1891. Initially, the damp, leaking, and long-vacant president's house had no beds. After being repaired and carpeted, the house was soon replaced by a new $4,500 structure. When it was discovered that the institution account was overdrawn by almost $6,500, the new president was designated as treasurer by the college.

During the fall term of 1891, Ross was often seen strolling the campus and befriending the cadets. Once he "got hold of the reins," Sul described his job as agreeable and pleasant. During this session thirteen more faculty and staff from the McInnis era were dropped, while ten new members were added and five were given new assignments. A new three-story dormitory (Ross Hall) was built, and a precision drill team from the cadet corps was renamed the Ross Volunteers.

Under the new administration, the minimum age for enrollment dropped from sixteen to fifteen. All new students were interviewed by President Ross, and they had to deposit their firearms and deadly weapons with him. Students were then sent to professors for class enrollment and to the commandant for assignment to cadet companies and quarters. There were two main courses of study, agricultural and mechanical, and four possible degrees: bachelor of scientific agriculture or scientific horticulture, and bachelor of mechanical engineering or civil engineering. Extra hours were added in grammar, the sciences, math, and history, making a total of twenty-eight hours a week each term. Hazing was officially prohibited.

External criticism orchestrated by two former A&M professors led to the stormiest period in Ross's presidency. After losing the faculty chairmanship and being forced into retirement, the embittered Professor McInnis made a fruitless effort to have state senator Henry A. Finch conduct a legislative investigation of the A&M situation. McInnis then found a better ally in a former colleague, Dr. J. D. Read, college physician and instructor of physiology until he was fired. Reviving memories of the Civil War and Reconstruction, Dr. Read came to the public's attention by asserting that *Southern* men should replace the two "Northern Republicans" from Iowa who had recently joined the A&M faculty.

The controversy widened when President Ross became involved in the 1892 gubernatorial campaign. Incumbent Jim Hogg was opposed in the race by the candidate of his enemies, the respected Waco attorney, George Clark. Sul chose to back Clark, his old friend and former campaign manager, rather than Hogg, whom he had earlier characterized as being "bull-headed." Ross was in a sensitive position to incur the wrath of a sitting governor and ruefully admitted that "if Hogg gets in again, he will probably decapitate me." After a very spirited campaign, Jim was reelected governor with 190,480 votes to Clark's 133,395.

In late January 1893, an article in the *Texas Farmer* took A&M to task for imparting theoretical, not practical, knowledge to its students. Furthermore, it was asserted that the college had an overpaid president who was really an "avowed corporation politician." A month later, an open letter in the *Galveston Daily News* condemned the excessive cost of attending A&M, and demanded the creation of student jobs to help pay expenses.

Official hostile scrutiny of the college came early in Governor Hogg's second term when a five-man legislative visitation committee — three representatives and two senators — was appointed to inspect five state institutions. President Ross contended that these Hogg men were poisoned against the college when they arrived but left "converted." However, A&M was the only school singled out for detailed — and negative — comment by the visiting committee. Their partisan report took note of poor food service and laundry work, ever-increasing salaries, and a management seeking to divert A&M from its purpose; i.e., to convert it from an industrial to a military and literary school. The report was sweet revenge to the pleased Dr. Read, who said it was a stab at the college.

Despite this adverse publicity, President Ross continued to enjoy broad public support; in fact, the 1893 fall enrollment at A&M jumped to 343 students. From then on, Sul was forced to announce that the school was at capacity on the first day of each fall session. By his last year in office, the president was requiring parents to write him before sending their sons to A&M.

From the fall of 1891 until the fall of 1898, the college spent almost $100,000 on improvements and new construction, including a new mess hall that seated 500 students. A surplus in the treasury enabled the school to cut student costs and to initiate a new student job program.

The president defined the college chain of command and persuaded the board of directors to adopt provisions linking tenure of office with "good behavior and efficiency of service." Under the new regime, administrators and faculty could not be dismissed without reasonable notice. Ross was very accessible to the student body, even to the point of seeing to their financial and personal needs. Each month he inspected, signed, and wrote comments on the grade sheets of each student. Poor grades could result in a personal admonition from the president. He also addressed an attentive cadet corps during morning chapel services, offering advice and instruction based on the Bible and a wealth of personal experience. The cadets loved, and were in awe of, this legendary figure out of the Texas past, a role model who never used profanity or showed anger.

President Ross embued Texas A&M with its patriotic military traditions, but literary groups and the Young Men's Christian Association also flourished during his presidency. Two societies, the Calliopean and the Austin, published a literary magazine, the *College Journal,* until 1893. In that year the more newspaperlike *Battalion* supplanted it. For years the paper's masthead carried these words of tribute: "Lawrence Sullivan Ross — Soldier, Statesman, Knightly Gentleman." Football was first played at A&M in 1894, while the first college annual, *The*

Olio, appeared in 1895. The president personally favored coeducation — but to no avail. Indeed, women were a rare sight on the A&M campus in the 1890s.

After Charles A. Culberson was elected governor of Texas in 1894, he appointed Sul to a seat on the Railroad Commission. Ross gave serious thought to resigning and accepting the new position until a flood of petitions and letters persuaded him to stay at A&M. In both 1893 and 1894, Ross was elected commander of the Texas Division of United Confederate Veterans. Before his death, four Confederate veteran camps were named in his honor.

Sul remained an outdoorsman all his life and loved to camp out while hunting and fishing. During the college Christmas vacation of 1897–98, he and his son Neville joined some friends for ten days of deer and turkey hunting in the Navasota River bottoms. During one cold, rainy chase, the elder Ross overexerted himself, then ate some undercooked biscuits and sausage. After developing a severe chill and acute indigestion, Sul drove home alone in his buckboard. He was deathly sick when he went to bed on Thursday evening, December 30. The family was called in after the fifty-nine-year-old Ross suffered an episode of "acute congestion of the stomach and bowels" about 5:00 that Sunday afternoon. He died peacefully at 6:35 P.M. on Monday, January 3, 1898. There was no death certificate, but evidence points to a coronary heart attack as the probable cause of death.[4]

The following tribute appeared in the *Dallas Morning News* the morning after his death:

---

[4] This explanation of Ross's death is disputed in *Rangers of Texas* by Roger N. Conger, et al. According to this account, Sul was accidentally poisoned during the hunting trip. It seems that since the camp area along the Navasota River was full of wood rats, the Negro cook had brought along some white rat poison that resembled flour. Somehow a portion of the rat poison got into the wooden flour barrel. After the cook baked a batch of hot biscuits from this tainted flour, all of the hunting party became seriously ill, but only Ross died from eating the poisoned biscuits. Sul's descendants give little credence to this fascinating story.

It has been the lot of few men to be of such great service to Texas as Sul Ross . . . Throughout his life he . . . discharged every duty imposed upon him with diligence, ability, honesty, and patriotism . . . He was not a brilliant chieftain in the field, nor was he masterful in the art of politics, but, better than either, he was a well-balanced, well-rounded man from whatever standpoint one might estimate him . . . He leaves a name that will be honored as long as chivalry, devotion to duty and spotless integrity are standards of our civilization, and an example which ought to be an inspiration to all young men of Texas who aspire to careers of public usefulness and honorable renown.

The entire A&M student body escorted Ross's remains back to Waco, where Confederate veterans dressed in faded gray served as his honor guard. With a throng of 5,000 friends and admirers looking on, he was buried near his father Shapley in the Ross plot at Oakwood Cemetery. His modest gravestone bears this inscription: "Lawrence Sullivan Ross. Sept. 27, 1838. Jan. 3, 1898." There are no references to his public life; the name is fame enough.

Sul Ross has not been forgotten by the people of Texas. In 1917, the state legislature appropriated $10,000 for a suitable memorial. The ten-foot bronze statue by Pompeo Coppini was unveiled on May 4, 1919, and now stands in front of the Academic Building on the campus of Texas A&M. A focal point of campus life, this statue of "Sully" is kept scrubbed and polished by A&M freshmen. The Ross Volunteers, that precision drill team named for a beloved president, has a statewide reputation for excellence. The pioneer educator received yet another honor when the Thirty-fifth Legislature established Sul Ross Normal College at Alpine in 1917. This teacher-training institution opened its doors in June 1920, and is now Sul Ross State University.

Sul Ross as a teenager.
— Courtesy The Texas
Collection, Baylor University

Sul Ross as a Confederate
brigadier general.
— Courtesy University Archives,
Sterling C. Evans Library,
Texas A&M University

Sul Ross as president of
Texas A&M College.
— Courtesy University Archives,
Sterling C. Evans Library,
Texas A&M University

Ross bronze statue on the
Texas A&M campus.
— Courtesy University Archives,
Sterling C. Evans Library,
Texas A&M University

Sul Ross's home while president of Texas A&M College. The
structure burned in the mid 1960s.
— Courtesy University Archives, Sterling C. Evans
Library, Texas A&M University

Texas A&M College campus about 1895, with Old Main on
the left and Ross Hall on the right.
— Courtesy University Archives, Sterling C. Evans
Library, Texas A&M University

193

Suggested Sources
for Further Reading

I
"Three-Legged Willie" Williamson:
A Legend in His Own Time

Anderson, John Q., ed. *Tales of Frontier Texas, 1830–1860.* Dallas: Southern Methodist University Press, 1966.

Barker, Eugene C., ed. Francis White Johnson's *A History of Texas and Texans, By . . . A Leader in the Texas Revolution.* 5 vols. Chicago and New York: The American Historical Society, 1914.

Brown, John Henry. *Life and Times of Henry Smith.* Dallas: A. D. Aldridge and Co., 1887.

Davis, Robert E., ed. *Diary of William Barret Travis.* Waco: Texian Press, 1966.

Holley, Mrs. Mary (Austin). *Texas.* fac. Austin: Steck Co., 1935.

McDonald, Archie. *Travis.* Austin: Jenkins Publishing Co., 1976.

Ray, Worth S. *Austin Colony Pioneers.* Austin: Jenkins Publishing Co., 1970.

"Robert M. Williamson." *Texas Almanac for 1861.* Galveston: Richardson and Co., 1860.

Robinson, Duncan W. *Judge Robert McAlpin Williamson: Texas' Three Legged Willie.* Austin: Texas State Historical Association, 1948.

Smith, Henry. "Reminiscences of Henry Smith." *Quarterly of the Texas State Historical Association* 14 (1910–1911).

Smithwick, Noah. *The Evolution of a State.* fac. Austin: Steck-Vaughn Co., 1968.

"Williamson Family of Georgia and Texas." *Southern Historical Research Magazine* 1 (April 1936).

II
Jack Hays:
He Fought the Good Fight

Anderson, John Q., ed. *Tales of Frontier Texas, 1830–1860*. Dallas: Southern Methodist University Press, 1966.

Barton, Henry W. *Texas Volunteers in the Mexican War*. Waco: Texian Press, 1970.

Brice, Donaly E. *The Great Comanche Raid: Boldest Indian Attack of the Texas Republic*. Austin: Eakin Press, 1987.

Conger, Roger, et al. *Rangers of Texas*. Waco: Texian Press, 1969.

Ford, John Salmon. Oates, Stephen B., ed. *Rip Ford's Texas*. Austin: University of Texas Press, 1963.

Grant, Ellsworth S. "Gunmaker to the World." (Samuel Colt). *American Heritage* (June 1968), 5–11, 86–91.

Greer, James K. *Colonel Jack Hays: Texas Frontier Leader and California Builder*. Rev. ed. College Station: Texas A&M University Press, 1987.

Mayhall, Mildred. *Indian Wars of Texas*. Waco: Texian Press, 1965.

Nance, Joseph Milton. *After San Jacinto: The Texas-Mexican Frontier, 1836–1841*. Austin: University of Texas Press, 1963.

———. *Attack and Counter-Attack: The Texas-Mexican Frontier, 1842*. Austin: University of Texas Press, 1964.

Nevin, David. *The Mexican War*. Alexandria, VA: Time-Life Books, 1978.

Syers, William. *Off the Beaten Trail*. Waco: Texian Press, 1971.

Webb, Walter Prescott. *The Texas Rangers: A Century of Frontier Defense*. 2nd ed. Austin: University of Texas Press, 1965.

III
Richard King:
Founder of a Ranching Empire

Broyles, William, Jr. "The Last Empire." (The King Ranch Saga) *Texas Monthly* (October 1980), 150–173, 234–278.

Dobie, J. Frank. *Cow People*. Boston: Little Brown, 1964.

————. *The Longhorns*. Boston: Little, 1941.

————. *Up the Trail From Texas*. New York: Random House, 1955.

————. *A Vaquero of the Brush Country*. Dallas: Southwest Press, 1929.

Douglas, C. L. *Cattle Kings of Texas*. Fort Worth: Branch-Smith, Inc., 1939.

Durham, George. *Taming the Nueces Strip: The Story of McNelly's Rangers*. Austin: University of Texas Press, 1962.

Frissell, Toni. *The King Ranch, 1939–1944; A Photographic Essay*. Published in cooperation with the Amon Carter Museum, Fort Worth. Dobbs Ferry, NY: Morgan & Morgan, 1975.

Goodwyn, Frank. *Life on the King Ranch*. New York: Thomas Y. Crowell, 1951.

Kleberg County Historical Commission. *Kleberg County, Texas*. Austin: Hart Graphics, 1979.

Lea, Tom. *The King Ranch*. 2 vols. Boston: Little, Brown and Co., 1957.

Nordyke, Lewis. *Great Roundup: The Story of Texas and Southwestern Cowmen*. New York: William Morrow & Co., 1955.

Oates, Stephen B., ed. *Rip Ford's Texas*. Austin: University of Texas Press, 1963.

Rister, Carl Coke. *Robert E. Lee in Texas*. Norman: University of Oklahoma Press, 1946.

Webb, Walter Prescott. *The Texas Rangers; A Century of Frontier Defense*. Austin: University of Texas Press, 1965.

Woodman, Lyman. *Cortina: Rogue of the Rio Grande*. San Antonio: Naylor, 1950.

IV
Sul Ross:
Warrior, Public Servant, and Educator

Benner, Judith Ann. *Sul Ross: Soldier, Statesman, Educator*. College Station: Texas A&M University Press, 1983.

Bolton, Paul. *Governors of Texas*. Corpus Christi: Caller-Times Pub. Co., 1947.

Burleson, Georgia J., comp. *The Life and Writings of Rufus C. Burleson, D. D., LL.D*. Waco: n.p., 1901.

Conger, Roger N. *Pictorial History of Waco*. Waco: Texian Press, 1964.

————, et al. *Rangers of Texas*. Waco: Texian Press, 1969.

DeShields, James T. *Cynthia Ann Parker: The Story of Her Capture*. 1886. Reprint. San Antonio: Naylor Co., 1934.

Dethloff, Henry C. *A Centennial History of Texas A&M University, 1876–1976*. 2 vols. College Station: Texas A&M University Press, 1975.

Jackson, Grace. *Cynthia Ann Parker*. San Antonio: Naylor Co., 1959.

Kelley, Dayton, ed. *The Handbook of Waco and McLennan County*. Waco: Texian Press, 1972.

Mayhall, Mildred. *Indian Wars of Texas*. Waco: Texian Press, 1965.

Nunn, William C., ed. *Ten More Texans in Gray*. Hillsboro, TX: Hill Junior College Press, 1980.

Oates, Stephen B., ed. *Rip Ford's Texas*. Austin: University of Texas Press, 1963.

Perry, George Sessions. *The Story of Texas A. and M.* New York: McGraw-Hill, 1951.

Preece, Harold. *Lone Star Man: Ira Aten; Last of the Old Texas Rangers*. New York: Hastings House, 1960.

Rose, Victor M. *Ross' Texas Brigade: Being a Narrative of Events Connected with Its Service in the Late War Between the States*. 1881. Reprint. Kennesaw, GA: Continental Book Co., 1960.

Simpson, Harold B. *Cry Comanche; the 2nd U.S. Cavalry in Texas, 1855–1861*. Hillsboro, TX: Hill Junior College Press, 1979.

Sleeper, John, and J. C. Hutchins, comps. *Waco and McLennan County, Texas, 1876*. Reprint. Waco: Texian Press, 1966.

Sowell, A. J. *History of Fort Bend County*. Houston: W. H. Coyle & Co., 1904.

Welch, June Rayfield. *The Glory That Was Texas*. Dallas: G. L. A. Press, 1975.

————. *The Texas Governor*. Dallas: G. L. A. Press, 1977.

Wharton, Clarence. *History of Fort Bend County*. San Antonio: Naylor Co., 1939.

Yelderman, Pauline. *The Jay Bird Democratic Association of Fort Bend County; A White Man's Union*. Waco: Texian Press, 1979.

198

Index

A

Adelsverein, 51
Agaton (bandit), 49
Agricultural and Mechanical
College of Texas (*see*
Texas A&M College)
Agua Dulce, 105, 119
Aitken, John, 6
Allen, Professor, 119
Allsens, Adam, 69
Allsopp, J. P., 82
Alvarado, Francisco, 109
Ignacio, 125f
Ramón, 129
American Flag, 93
American Quarter Horse As-
sociation, 140
Ampudia, Pedro de, 56, 58,
59, 60
Anahuac, 6–9, 13
Anahuac Insurrection, 3f
Anderson, Reverend Doctor,
64
Antonio, 111
Archer, Branch T., 14
Arista, General, 55
Armstead (slave), 151
Armstrong, John B., 140
Army of Northern Virginia,
170
Ashbrook, Pearl, 123, 130
"Assault," 139

Aten, Ira, 178–179, 180–182
Atwood, E. B., 123
Nettie, 138
Austin, John T., 9
Stephen F., 2, 5, 6, 9, 11–
12, 14
Austin Democrat, 75
Austin Society, 189
Ayish District, 3f

B

Bagdad, 106, 107, 108, 112
Baker, Mosely, 127f
Banks, Nathaniel, 108
Barry, Buck, 57
Bassett, Clem, 182
Bastrop, Baron de, 2
Battalion, 189
Battle of Antelope Hills, 154
Battle of Bandera Pass, 39
Battle of Franklin, 168
Battle of Gonzales, 14
Battle of the Llano, 39
Battle of Painted Rock, 52
Battle of Pea Ridge, 165
Battle of Pease River, 158–
162
Battle of Plum Creek, 35
Battle of Richmond, 181
Battle of Salado, 44
Battle of San Jacinto, 18, 32
Battle of Walker's Creek, 50

199

Battle of Wichita Village,
156
Baylor, John R., 158
Baylor University at Independence, 152
Beauregard, P. G. T., 166
Bee, Hamilton, 108
Bell, Peter H., 65
Benavides, Santos, 109
Benton, Thomas Hart, 63
Bessie, 112
Bibbs, W. H., 19f
Bigfoot, 150
Big House, 134, 138
Billingsley, Walter, 130
Birdsong, Neda Parker, 161f
Bishop's Palace, 58, 59
Boca del Rio, 91, 93
Bogart, Samuel, 47
Brackett, Albert, 66
Bradburn, John Davis, 7–9
Brazos Agency, 153
Brazos Santiago, 112
Brenham Grays, 181
Bridge, Samuel, 2
Briscoe, Andrew, 13
Brown, Henry S., 40f
Brownsville Town Company,
94
Bryant, J. J., 79
Buchanan, James, 83
John, 65
Buell, Don Carlos, 166
Buffalo Hump, 35, 49, 154,
155, 156
Burleson, Edward, 46
Rufus C., 152
Burnet, David G., 10
Byron, Lord, 4

C
Caddo Indians, 154
Caddo John, 157

Cage, Robert, 31
Caldwell, Matthew "Old
Paint," 43, 44–46
William, 180
Calliopean Society, 189
Calvert, Jeremiah H., 49
Susan, 49, 54, 64
Camargo, 111
Camp Chacon, 47
Camp Cooper, 162
Camp Radziminski, 155, 157,
158
Cantu, Juan, 99
Caperton, John, 77, 78, 79
Capitol Board, 177
Carroll, Judge, 131
Castro, Henri, 51
Cavalry of the West, 109
Cavazos, Bobby, 100f
Lauro, 100f
Richard, 100f
Centre College, 105
Centre Presbyterian College,
120
Chamberlain, Bland, 119
Caroline, 116f
Edwin, 119
Henrietta Maria Morse,
95–96, 100 (*see also*
King, Henrietta)
Hiram, 95, 96, 105, 108,
119
Hiram, Jr., 119
Samuel, 55
Willie, 119
Chamberlain Cemetery, 138
Chamberlain Park, 138
Champion, 90, 91
Chapman, W. W., 102
Chevaille, Mike, 38, 54, 62,
72, 81
Citadel, 56

Clark, Edward, 163, 164
  George, 175, 188
Clement, James H., 140
Clopper, J. C., 3
Coast Rangers, 82
Coffee, John, 31
Coke, Richard, 115, 131
Coleman, John, 49
  Robert, 14
College Journal, 189
Collins Station, 123
Colonel Cross, 92–93, 94
Colonel Fremont, 79
Colonization Law of 1830, 6, 7
Colt, Samuel, 40–41, 62, 63
Colt revolvers, 49–51, 62–63f, 65
Comanche, 94, 96
Comanches, 33, 34–37, 39–40, 41, 49, 50–51, 52–53, 149, 150, 153–156, 159–162
Commissioner of the Land Office, 177
"Committee of Vigilance of San Francisco," 79
Comstock Lode, 83
Confederate Conscription Act, 165
Conger, Roger N., 190f
Conner, John, 76
Constitution of 1824, 13, 15
Constitutional Convention of 1875, 173
Convention of 1833, 9, 11
Cooper and Cheeves, 3
Coppini, Pompeo, 191
Cordova, Jacob de, 151
Corley, Samuel H., 75
Corning, A. F., 161f

Corpus Christi, San Diego & Rio Grande Narrow Gauge Railroad, 123, 136f
Corpus Christi Free Press, 122
Corpus Christi Gazette, 118
Corpus Christi Navigation Company, 122
Cortina, Juan, 103, 108, 114
Corvette, 91, 92
Cos, Martín Perfecto de, 13–14
Cotten, Godwin B., 4, 5
Council House Fight, 34
Culberson, Charles A., 190
Cureton, J. H. (Jack), 159, 162
Curtis, Samuel R., 164
Cushing, Caleb, 65
Cuthbert's Seminary, 120, 123

D
Daggett, Ephraim, 70
Dallas Herald, 170
Dallas Morning News, 190
Dana, N. J. T., 108
Davidson Academy, 31
Davis, "Alligator," 36f
  Henry Clay, 93
  Jefferson, 184f
de la Garza Santa Gertrudis grant, 98, 102, 105
Delaware Indians, 34, 154
Department of the Brazos, 12
Department of the Interior, 78
Desdemona, 90
De Witt, Green, 6
Díaz, Porfirio, 116
Dickson, David C., 26
Dinsmore, Silas, 10

Dobie, J. Frank, 120, 125f
Donahoe, Isaac, 32
Driscoll, Robert, 136
Driskill Hotel, 176
Duran, José, 73
Durham, George, 116

E
Edwards, Gustavus E., 22, 27
    Mary Jane, 22
    Monroe, 8
Elleard, Charles M., 80
Elliot, Eleanor, 46
El Primero, 111
El Sauz rancho, 116f
Enchanted Rock, 40, 52
Enterprise, 111
Erath, George B., 150
Eugenia, 111
Evans, Mrs., 162
    Nathan G., 159

F
Farmers' Alliance, 175
Federation Hill, 56, 58
Fernwood ranch, 83
Finch, Henry A., 187
First Regiment, Texas
    Mounted Volunteers, 54,
    65
Fisher, William S., 48
Fitch, John, 118
Flacco, 34, 37, 39, 46, 48
Flores, Juan, 116
Ford, John S. "Rip," 65, 66,
    68, 73, 74, 75, 98, 101,
    106, 109–110, 133, 153–
    154, 173
Fort Belknap, 153, 157, 159
Fort Bend County, 179, 182
Fort Brown, 108
Fort Leaton, 77
Fort Parker massacre, 162
Freaner, John, 85

Freeman, S. L., 168
Fremantle, ———, 107
Fremont, John C., 164
Frisco Railroad, 135
Frost, Henry H. "Red Hot,"
    181

G
Galveston Daily News, 175,
    185, 188
Galveston News, 176
Garcia, Ignacio, 38
Garvey, Jim, 180, 181
Gates, John W., 178
Gathright, T. S., 184f
Giant, 139
Gibbons, Emory, 53
Gibson, Guilf, 180–181
    Ned, 180
    Volney, 180–181
Giddings, Luther, 61
Gila Apaches, 78–79
Gillespie, Ad, 49, 50, 58, 59
Goodnight, Charles, 130
Governor's Mansion, 177
Grampus, 94, 96
Granite Club, 81
Gray, William Fairfax, 16
Green, Tom, 128f
Grimes, Jesse, 24
Griswold, Anna Adelia, 95f
Guerrero, Mexico, 47–48

H
Halsell, W. E., 125
Hancock, Mr., 129
Harney, General, 78
Harrison, F. W., 53
Hatch, Edward, 168
Hays, Alex, 71
    Bob, 80
    Elizabeth, 83
    Harmon, 31
    Jack, 150

John Caperton, 80, 83
  Robert, 30–31
  Sarah, 31
  Susan, 80, 83 (*see also* Calvert, Susan)
Henderson, J. Pinckney, 54, 63
Henderson Female Institute, 119
Henrietta M. King High School, 137
Hereford cattle, 135
Herff, Ferdinand, 132, 133
Hermitage, 31
Herron, Francis J., 109
Highsmith, Samuel, 76, 78
Hitchcock, Ethan Allen, 68
Hogg, James S., 183–184, 186, 188
Holland, Joe, 90
Holman, Lucius, 185
Hood, John Bell, 170
Horton, A. C., 62
Houston, Margaret Lea, 177
  Sam, 9, 14, 15, 16, 17, 25, 26, 32, 33, 45–46, 48, 127f, 158, 159, 161, 162, 163, 177
  Temple, 177
Houston & Texas Central Railway, 178
Houston Light Guard, 181
Howard, John, 38
  Volney E., 24
Hubbard, Richard B., 116f
Hudson, Sarah, 2
Hughes, George W., 73
Humble Oil and Refining Company, 139
Humphreys, P. W., 69
Hunter, David, 164
  Jack, 77

Huntington, Collis P., 183
Huston, Felix, 35

I
Independence Baptist Church, 152
Independence Hill, 56, 58, 59
Ireland, Governor, 178
Isbell, Branch, 120

J
Jack, Patrick, 7–9, 10
  William, 10
Jackson, Andrew, 31
  Rachel Donelson, 31
  William H. "Red," 167, 168
James, James Garland, 184f
  Jesse, 132f
James Hale, 108
James-Younger gang, 132f
Jarauta, Padre Celedonia de, 70, 71–72
Jaybird-Woodpecker War, 179–183
Jayhawkers, 164
Jenkins, John, 79
  John H., Sr., 17
Jett, Stephen, 44
Johnson, Francis W., 3, 8, 15
  Lyndon, 138
  Middleton T., 158
Johnston, Albert Sidney, 165
  Joseph E., 168, 169
Jones, Anson, 51
  Frank, 180
  J. W., 25

K
Karnes, Henry, 33
Kelliher, Thomas, 160, 161
Kelly, William, 112
Kenedy, James, 133

Mifflin, 90–91, 93, 94, 96, 103, 105, 111, 112–113, 115, 121, 122, 126, 129, 133, 136f, 138
Petra, 133
Kenedy Pasture Company, 129
Kenly, John R., 73–74
Kerr, James, 15
Kineños, 99–100, 101, 125, 132, 138
King, Alice Gertrudis, 106, 119, 120, 123, 127–128, 130, 132 (*see also* Kleberg, Alice)
Ella Morse, 103, 119, 123, 138
"Fiddling Jim," 178
General, 61
Henrietta, 109, 119, 124, 132, 133, 137–138
Henrietta Marie ("Nettie"), 102, 119, 123
Kenedy & Co., 111
Richard II, 106, 119, 120, 123, 125f, 130
Richard III, 132
Richard, Jr., 138
Robert E. Lee, 109, 119, 120, 128, 138
W. H., 180
King Ranch (*see* Chapter III)
King Ranch, Inc., 140
Kingsville, Texas, 98, 137
Kinney, Henry Lawrence, 96
Kleberg, Alice, 134, 138
Helen, 139, 140
Otto, 128f
Richard Mifflin, 138
Robert, 104
Robert, Jr., 138–140
Robert Justus I, 126f

Robert Justus II, 126, 128f, 133, 134, 135, 138, 140
Rosalie, 127f
Rudolph, 128f
Stephen J. "Tio," 140
Kleberg County, 137
Kleberg County Courthouse, 104
Kleberg Town and Improvement Company, 137
Knights of Labor, 175, 178
Know-Nothing Party, 26

L
Labadie, Dr., 18
Lamar, Mirabeau B., 18, 23, 36, 38, 42
Lane, Joseph "Jo," 66, 67, 70–71, 72
La Parra grant, 129
Laredo Expedition, 33
Laredo, Texas, 32–33, 37, 46–47
Laureles grant, 112
Leal, Manuel, 38
Leaton, Ben, 77
Lee, Robert E., 103, 169, 170
Lemon, Elizabeth, 6
Lewis, Gideon K. "Legs," 97–99, 102
Lindsay, James, 8
Line of the Bravo, 114, 116
Linn, John Joseph, 35
Linnville, 35
Lipan Indians, 34, 46
Lockhart, Matilda, 34
Logan, William, 7
Lone Star Fair, 96, 97
Long, Jane, 3–4
Long Quiet, 50
Lorenzo (Mexican guide), 76, 77
Los Laureles ranch, 129, 138

Lott, Cicele, 137f
  Uriah, 136
Lubbock, Francis, 169
M
M. Kenedy & Co., 96, 107, 108, 110, 111
McCulloch, Ben, 44, 54, 55, 57, 164
  Henry E., 36, 41, 43, 46
McGuire, Mrs., 119
McInnis, Louis Lowry, 185, 186, 187
McManus, ——, 172
McMullin, Anna, 83
  John, 50
McNamara, J. S., 136f
McNelly, L. H., 115–116
Magruder, John, 109
Major, James P., 156
Marcy, William, 64, 78
Maria Burt, 75
Martin, Marion, 178
  Wylie, 14
Martinez, Anton, 161
Matamoros Expedition, 3f
Matamoros, Mexico, 54
Maury, Dabney H., 166, 167
Maverick, Mary, 35
  Samuel, 35, 76, 77
Mayfield, James, 45
Memphis and Charleston Railroad, 166
Mendiola, Juan, 98
Menger Hotel, 124, 133
Mescalero Apaches, 77
Mexia, General, 177
  José, 8
Mexican Citizen, 6
Mexican National Railway, 123, 136f
Mexico City, Mexico, 68, 69
"Middleground," 139

Mier Expedition, 48
Mier, Mexico, 48
Milam, Ben, 6, 23
Miller, J. H. C., 12
  James F., 131
Missouri-Pacific railroad, 137
Mobile Register and Advertiser, 168
"Modocs," 172
Mohee, 156
"Monkey," 139
Monroe, Daniel, 149
  Hugh, 90
Monterrey, Mexico, 56, 58–61
Monumental Fire Company, 80
Moore, John H., 14
Morgan Line Steamers, 122
Morning Star, 51
Morrill Act, 184f
Morse, Maria, 95f
Mountain Home Ranch, 80
Musquiz, Ramón, 10
Mustang, 108
N
Najera, Juan, 57
National Cattle Trail, 131
National City Bank of New York, 111
National Hotel, 181
National Stockmen's Convention, 130
Navarro County Fence War, 179
Neil, J. W., 133
New Orleans Picayune, 75
New Orleans Times Democrat, 129
Nicholson, I. D., 85
"Nokoni's Joe," 161f

205

O

Oakland Gas Light Company, 84
Oakland Light Cavalry, 85
Oakwood Cemetery, 191
Ocean, 127f
Ocean View School District, 84
O'Donnell, James, 94
"Old Sorrel," 140
Olio, 190
Ormsby, William, 83

P

Padre Island, 119
Paiute Indians, 83–84
Palmer-Sullivan Syndicate, 136f
Paredes, Mariano, 71
Parker, Cynthia Ann, 148, 160–162
　Isaac, 162
　J. W., 180–181
　Pecos, 162
　Quanah, 161f, 162
Parker's Fort, 14
Patterson, Robert, 66
Pease, Elisha M., 26
Peralta, Luis, 80
　Vicente, 80
Perez, Captain, 43
Peta Nacona, 154, 159, 161
Peyton, Jonathan C., 3, 6–7
　Mrs., 7
Piedras, José de las, 9
Pierce, Franklin, 81
　Shanghai, 130
Placido, 153
Plum, Lewis, 6
Pohebits Quasho (or Iron Jacket), 154
Polk, James K., 52, 60, 63, 65, 71

Sarah Childress, 63
William H., 71
Powers, Stephen, 121
Presidio del Norte, 77
Price, Sterling, 164, 166
public school lands, 175

Q

Quinoñes, Agatón, 37

R

R. King & Co., 105, 111, 112, 113
Railroad Commission, 190
Rancho Puerta de Agua Dulce, 130
Rangers of Texas, 190f
Rawlinson, Willie, 126
Rea, General, 67
Read, J. D., 187–188
Redland Company, 18
Reservation War, 158
Reyes, Isidro, 46
Rice, Septimus P., 153
Richardson, James, 99, 108–109, 114
Richmond Examiner, 81
Riddle, Elizabeth, 54
Rincon de Santa Gertrudis grant, 98, 105, 118, 119, 121
Ringling Brothers, 140
Rio Grande Female Institute, 95
Rio Grande Railroad Company, 111
Roberts, Jacob, 67, 69
　Oran, 185f
Robertson Colony, 149
Robinson, James W., 19f
Roeder, Rosalie von, 127f
　Rudolf von, 127f
Rose, Mrs. Pleasant W., 11
　Pleasant W., 10

Victor M., 174, 175
Rosecrans, William S., 166
Ross, Catherine Fulkerson, 149, 171
    Elizabeth, 168, 174
    Kate, 151
    Lizzie, 171
    Mervin, 171
    Neville, 190
    "Pease," 162
    Peter, 151, 163, 164, 171, 172, 173
    Shapley P., 148–151, 153, 171, 177, 191
Ross Hall, 187
Ross Volunteers, 187, 191
Rusk, Thomas J., 22, 32, 127f

S

Sabine, 127f
St. Louis, Brownsville & Mexican Railroad, 136, 137f
San Antonio and Aransas Pass Railway, 136–137f
Sanders, John, 91
San Diego, 119
San Felipe de Austin, 2–3
San Fernando de Rosas, 46
San Juan de Carricitos grant, 113, 119
San Salvador del Tule grant, 105
Santa Anna, 12–13, 70, 73–74
Santa Fe Expedition, 23, 42
Santa Gertrudis cattle, 139, 140
Saus Creek, 119
Scott, Winfield, 64, 66, 69, 70, 92, 157
Seguin, Juan, 38, 42
Sesma, General, 17

Shamblin, J. M., 180
Sheriff's Association of Texas, 172
Shorthorn cattle, 135, 171
Sieker, L. P., 179
Smith, Ashbel, 20–21
    Ben Fort, 10
    Erastus "Deaf," 32–33
    Giles S., 110
    Henry, 12, 15
    J. M., 158
    John W., 43
    William H., 18
Smithwick, Noah, 2, 4–5, 17, 18
Socie, John, 159
Solms-Braunfels, Prince Carl of, 51
Somervell, Alexander, 46–48
Southern Pacific Railroad, 135, 137f, 181, 183
Spangler, John W., 159
Sparks, William, 2
Specht, Franz, 115
Speed, James, 108–109
Spencer, U. C., 163
Star, Belle, 172
State Cemetery, 27
State Land Board, 175
Stevens, James H., 117
Stillman, Charles "Carlos," 94, 96, 111, 112
Stock Raisers Association of Western Texas, 115
Stone, B. Warren, 164
Storey, Edward, 83
Stuart, John (*see* Socie, John)
Sul Ross State University, 191
Swain, William J., 175, 176
Swenson, S. M., 41

207

T

Tamaulipas, 111
Taylor, Zachary, 52, 54, 55, 60, 61, 91, 92
Tehuacana Indians, 14
Telegraph and Texas Register, 41
Tennessee campaign, 170
Tenorio, Antonio, 13
Terry, Kyle, 180
Texas A&M College, 148, 184–191
Texas Banner, 20
Texas Cavalry Brigade, 167–168, 170
Texas Centennial Commission, 27
Texas Division of United Confederate Veterans, 190
Texas Farmer, 188
Texas Gazette, 5
Texas Land & Cattle Co., Ltd., 129
Texas Mexican Railway Company, 123, 136f
Texas Military Institute, 184f
Texas navy, 23–24, 49
Texas Ranger, 26, 27
Texas Rangers, 1, 16, 115, 131, 151 (*see* Chapter II)
Texas Republican, 6
Texas State Fair, 161f
Third Texas Cavalry, 169
Tilden, Samuel J., 84
Tinsley, David Augustus, 163
  Elizabeth Dorothy, 157, 163
Tonkawas, 154
Torrey, David K., 41

Travis, William Barret, 1, 6–9, 10, 11, 12, 16
Trimble, R. C., 33
Trueheart, ——, 39
Truett, A. M., 65, 72, 74
Turtle Bayou Resolutions, 8

U

U.S. Department of Agriculture, 139
Union National Bank, 84
Union Savings Bank, 84
University of California, 82
University of Texas, 184f
Urrea, José, 3f

V

Van Dorn, Earl, 154–157, 165, 166–167, 168
Vasquez, Rafael, 42
Vega, Tomás de la, 172
Victoria Advocate, 174
Vidal, Petra Vela de, 96
Viesca, Augustín, 12
Virginia City Rifles, 83

W

Waco Daily Examiner, 172, 175, 176
Walker, Samuel, 48, 51, 54, 58, 62
Wallace, Benjamin Rush, 25 Bigfoot, 36, 48
Walworth, James, 102, 105, 111
  Jane, 111
Ward, J. F., 157
Washoe Regiment, 84
Wells, James B. "Jim," 121–122, 132
Welton, Louis M., 123
Wesleyan University, 152–153, 157
West, Sheriff, 178
Wharton, John A., 14–15

William H., 9
Wheeler, Thomas B., 183
White, Walter, 3
White Man, 158
Whiteville, 94–95
Whitfield, John W., 168, 169, 173
Whiting, Henry, 55–56
Whitney, Eli, Jr., 63f
Wild Horse Desert, 91, 97, 115
Williams, Samuel May, 6
Williamson, Ann McAlpin, 1–2
  Hoxie Collingsworth, 23
  Julia Rebecca, 23
  Mary Jane, 26
  Micajah, 1
  Peter B., 1–2
  Willie Annexus, 23, 24

"Wimpy P-1," 140
Winnemucca, 84
Woll, Adrian, 42–45
Wood, George T., 54, 78
Woodruff, Mr., 11
Worth, William, 56–57, 58–59, 61

Y
Yarrington, J. T., 102
Yelderman, Pauline, 183
Yellowstone, 18
Yellow Wolf, 50
Yoakum, B. F., 135, 136f
  Henderson, 1
Young Men's Christian Association, 189
Young Men's Democratic Club, 180
Yturri, Mrs., 38

Z
Zavala, Lorenzo de, 14